POWER PRINCIPLES

THE BENEFITS OF A WISDOM-DRIVEN LIFE

DALE C. BRONNER

WHITAKER
HOUSE

Unless otherwise indicated, all Scripture quotations are taken from the *New King James Version*, © 1979, 1980, 1982, 1984 by Thomas Nelson, Inc. Used by permission. Scripture quotations are taken from the *Holy Bible, New International Version*®, NIV®, © 1973, 1978, 1984, 2011 by Biblica, Inc.® Used by permission of Zondervan. All rights reserved worldwide. www.zondervan.com. The "NIV" and "New International Version" are trademarks registered in the United States Patent and Trademark Office by Biblica, Inc.® Scripture quotations marked (KJV) are taken from the King James Version of the Holy Bible.

Italics in Scripture quotations indicate the author's emphasis.

The quote about Bernard of Chartres in the Acknowledgments is taken from Daniel Doyle MacGarry, ed., *The Metalogicon of John Salisbury: A Twelfth-century Defense of the Verbal and Logical Arts of the Trivium*, trans. by Daniel Doyle MacGarry (Berkeley: University of California Press, 1955), 167. See https://books.google.com/books?id=pA3VbvUf67EC&lpg.

POWER PRINCIPLES:
The Benefits of a Wisdom-Driven Life

Dale C. Bronner
212 Riverside Pkwy
Austell, GA 30168
contact@woffamily.org
www.woffamily.org

Hardcover edition ISBN: 978-1-62911-800-0
International trade paperback edition ISBN: 978-1-62911-881-9
eBook ISBN: 978-1-62911-801-7
Printed in the United States of America
© 2017 by Dale C. Bronner

Whitaker House
1030 Hunt Valley Circle
New Kensington, PA 15068
www.whitakerhouse.com

Library of Congress Cataloging-in-Publication Data (Pending)

1 2 3 4 5 6 7 8 9 10 11 12 ⨃ 25 24 23 22 21 20 19 18 17

ACKNOWLEDGMENTS

John of Salisbury wrote, "Bernard of Chartres used to compare us to dwarfs perched on the shoulders of giants. He pointed out that we see more and farther than our predecessors, not because we have keener vision or greater height, but because we are lifted up and borne aloft on their gigantic stature." So I share the sentiments of Sir Isaac Newton who, apparently being inspired by these words, said, "If I have seen further, it is by standing upon the shoulders of giants."

I am deeply grateful for the giants in my life who have helped me to see farther and have imparted their wisdom, encouragement, and support to me over the years. My father, Dr. Nathaniel Hawthorne Bronner Sr., was among the first of those giants. He was the wisest man I knew. His words of wisdom concerning life, money, business, health, people, and spirituality still echo in my heart. I am also eternally grateful for the wisdom that my godly mother imparted to me. I remember telling her once, "If you don't make it to heaven, no one is going to make it!"

I've had too many wonderful teachers and mentors over the years to mention here, but they all hold a special place of love and honor in my heart. I'm also deeply grateful to the amazing team of people at Whitaker House who have helped to make this book a reality. I am ultimately grateful for all the Holy Spirit has shared with me over the years. He is the Ancient of Days who reminds me that the wisdom of the ages is better than the knowledge of the moment.

—*Dale Carnegie Bronner*

CONTENTS

Foreword by John C. Maxwell 7

A Wisdom Legacy 9

Winning with Wisdom 12

PART ONE: THE WISDOM-DRIVEN LIFE

1. Wisdom Is the Principal Thing 21

2. Wisdom Leads Us to Our Purpose....................................30

3. Wisdom Trusts the Journey...44

PART TWO: WISDOM STRENGTHENS OUR POSITION

4. Wisdom Plans Ahead 55

5. Wisdom Creates Winning Habits, Part 1:
   The Power of Habit 69

6. Wisdom Creates Winning Habits, Part 2:
   Positive Practices for Success 79

7. Wisdom Develops Key Relationships, Part 1:
   The Power of Influence 92

8. Wisdom Develops Key Relationships, Part 2:
Cultivating Life Influences 100

9. Wisdom Teaches Your Dollars Some Sense, Part 1:
An Environment for Growth and Abundance.........................109

10. Wisdom Teaches Your Dollars Some Sense, Part 2:
Proven Financial Strategies 116

PART THREE: WISDOM CLEARS AWAY THE OBSTACLES

11. Wisdom Postpones Procrastination 133

12. Wisdom Gives Life Balance 148

13. Wisdom Is Content..162

14. Wisdom Releases the Negative and Promotes the Positive 175

PART FOUR: WISDOM FINISHES WELL

15. Wisdom Transforms Dreams to Reality......................189

16. Wisdom Leaves a Legacy...202

CONTINUING THE WISDOM-DRIVEN LIFE

Keep Seeking Wisdom 216

Use All the Sources of Wisdom 219

About the Author...224

FOREWORD

Many years ago, a friend asked me if I had a personal growth plan. At the time, I didn't even know that was something people designed for themselves. Were we supposed to formulate a *plan* for our personal development? Didn't positive growth just happen as we went along in life? Didn't we automatically mature with experience and age?

My friend's question set me on a new course in my life. I realized that if I was going to grow personally and professionally, I needed to become intentional about it. Since that time, I have been an avid student of personal development. I have benefitted in a multitude of ways from designing and following my own growth plan. But I have also seen how being purposeful about growth has transformed the lives of scores of people to whom I've had the privilege to teach life and leadership principles that I've learned and refined over the years. I've watched how their scope and influence have expanded and how their potential has been realized and borne fruit.

Intentionally focusing on personal and professional development enables us to discover our true purpose in life. To refine our gifts and skills. To see our dreams become reality. To accomplish our plans and goals. To develop our leadership ability. To live with greater internal integrity. What's more, as we focus on improving our own lives, we naturally influence the people and environments around us. We grow from our connections and interactions with others and learn how to build a better life together.

Power Principles: The Benefits of a Wisdom-Driven Life, by my friend Dale Bronner, presents a wide-ranging personal and professional growth plan in a single volume based on wisdom as the foundation for our lives. And what better foundation for personal development can we have than one built on time-tested wisdom applied to all areas of life? This book is packed with principles and insights for developing your full potential. It is the product of Dale's decades of personal experience, purposeful study, and application of what makes our lives successful, meaningful, and prosperous.

I have known Dale and his wife, Nina, for many years. Dale serves on the board of directors of my nonprofit organization EQUIP, which trains and mobilizes Christian leaders to impact families, organizations, communities, and nations around the world. We have spent much time together, and I know that he lives out the principles offered in this book.

To me, there's no goal more significant than helping people understand their purpose and potential. No matter what your personal or professional background, *Power Principles* will lead you into the benefits of wise and successful living as Dale discusses such topics as purpose, vision, process, planning, habits, relationships, mentorship, finances, attitudes, balance, resilience after failure, and leaving a strong legacy. He concludes with guidelines for continuing to pursue and apply wisdom as a lifelong quest with all the resources available to us.

You can lead a successful and fulfilling life while making a difference in the lives of those around you. But you do need to be purposeful about it—you do need a clear plan. Dale Bronner has provided you with a solid foundation for that plan in *Power Principles*. Absorb it. Follow it. Let it take you to greater heights. This book will enable you to release the fullness of your potential through the benefits and power of the wisdom-driven life.

—*John C. Maxwell*
New York Times best-selling author and speaker

A WISDOM LEGACY

I've always had a tremendous love for wisdom and been drawn to wisdom principles. At an early age, I was taught the value of wisdom by my parents, and that perspective has never failed me in good times or in difficult ones. My father, Mr. Nathaniel Hawthorne Bronner Sr., along with his brother, built a multimillion-dollar business, Bronner Brothers, from scratch. But the powerful principles he passed along to me and my five brothers were not only business secrets. They were wisdom secrets for success in all areas of life. I was taught principles such as:

- Success occurs when preparation meets opportunity.
- You only get one body, and a man will give all his money to regain his health, so preserve your health.
- Your judgment is no better than your information.
- There is no success that can compensate for failure at home.
- After you get your diploma, take it and throw it in the garbage can, roll up your sleeves, and go to work.
- The nerve that runs to the pocketbook is very sensitive.
- There is no discipline like the discipline of struggle.

+ "Let the words of my mouth, and the meditation of my heart, be acceptable in thy sight, O LORD, my strength, and my redeemer" (Psalm 19:14 KJV).

This background of wisdom principles gave me a solid foundation from which to gather wisdom from my own life experiences (both positive and negative); from the experiences of relatives, friends, and mentors; from my lifelong study of the Bible; and from the thoughts and writings of notable individuals throughout human history, a number of whom I quote in this book.

Because my family owned a company, I grew up in the business world and apparently wanted to begin my apprenticeship in learning business principles early. My very first job, which I began at the age of five, was delivering *The Atlanta Daily World* newspaper. By the time I was twelve, I was processing the payroll for my father's business. Over the years, I moved through a number of jobs within the company, including warehouse stock clerk, retail cashier, salesperson, accountant, purchasing director, and manager of information systems. Today, I am part owner of the company and serve on the board of directors.

I've also been involved in ministry on a weekly basis since the time I was fourteen. This corresponds with our family legacy of faith and of giving back to others, as reflected in the Bronner Brothers Mission Statement under "Our Community": "We will give back to the community in the form of charitable contributions, donations, moral support, and through the development of other entrepreneurs. We realize that this pursuit of excellence is a journey that we will unceasingly travel."

By the time I was sixteen, I was ministering monthly in a large prison and in four local convalescent homes. I was called to my first pastorate at age twenty-seven, and two years later, I founded Word of Faith Family Worship Cathedral, an interdenominational ministry that now has more than twenty thousand members. I am also the bishop of a network of sixteen thousand churches.

Today, I continue to have a number of roles in life, including businessman, bishop, civic leader, husband, and father. I have been in a variety of challenging places and faced many difficult times, as well as joyful and rewarding ones. While addressing the demands and opportunities of management, professional growth, and personal fulfillment, I have tested and applied many principles of wisdom. I am grateful that during this process—and as a result of it—I have been able to help thousands of people learn how to realize their maximum capacities by conveying these wisdom principles as a conference speaker, leadership trainer, pastor, and mentor. In *Power Principles: The Benefits of a Wisdom-Driven Life*, I share key foundational principles from the treasury of wisdom I have gathered for over forty years. I have a passion to develop the potential of leaders and others from all walks of life and to motivate them for success on the next level. I focus on practical strategies and proven techniques for finding and fulfilling your purpose, for relationship-building, for problem-solving, for creativity, for moving from ideas to implementation, and for leaving a legacy.

We never "arrive" when it comes to wisdom. Growing in wisdom is a process that continues in my life today and will for the rest of my time on earth. This is because wisdom is a journey, not a destination. We benefit from all the wisdom we accumulate and apply throughout each decade of life. Ralph Waldo Emerson said, "The years teach much which the days never knew." The wisdom we gain today often has immediate application, but it also can—and should—be stored in our minds and hearts for future use. Just as loving parents train their children when they are young, and provide them with instruction and caution for what they will encounter later in life, wisdom principles guide us for today's journey and also prepare us for much success and fulfillment in the future.

WINNING WITH WISDOM

John Naisbitt, author of the blockbuster book *Megatrends*, wrote in 1982, "We are drowning in information but starved for knowledge." There is much truth to this assertion, but I think that today, the reality has changed:

> We are devouring information and consuming knowledge—while starving for *wisdom*.

> Writer T. S. Eliot expressed a similar idea: "Where is the wisdom we have lost in knowledge? Where is the knowledge we have lost in information?"

We have unprecedented access to information and knowledge, but many problems continue to plague us personally and corporately because we have starved ourselves of the crucial component of wisdom—with all its benefits.

A WISDOM PROBLEM

It is widely recognized that there is a leadership crisis in our world. But we don't really have a leadership problem—we have a wisdom problem.

Many countries, businesses, and families struggle with unsound finances. But they don't really have a financial problem—they have a wisdom problem.

Every day, people suffer strained or broken relationships with family members, coworkers, neighbors, classmates, and others. But they don't really have a relationship problem—they have a wisdom problem.

In fact, we can trace every troubling contemporary issue to a lack of wisdom. Somehow, in the excitement and convenience of our Information Age, we have lost sight of this essential element of life. We benefit from the innumerable innovations and advancements that have developed from human knowledge and ingenuity. Information and creativity abound. However, not much true wisdom is being promoted in conjunction with their use. The world is filled with smart, educated people—but unfortunately relatively few wise people. More than a hundred and fifty years ago, writer and philosopher Thoreau warned, "Our inventions are [apt] to be pretty toys, which distract our attention from serious things. They are but improved means to an unimproved end, an end which it was already but too easy to arrive at."[1]

"THE ONLY MEDICINE FOR SUFFERING, CRIME, AND
ALL OTHER WOES OF MANKIND IS WISDOM."
—THOMAS HUXLEY

We might be unlocking the great secrets of the universe, but once we unlock them, we often don't know what to do with them, or we use them in a way that is counterproductive. Many things that humankind has discovered or devised have ended up turning against us. Isaac Asimov said, "The saddest aspect of life right now is that science gathers knowledge faster than society gathers wisdom."

---

1. Henry David Thoreau, *Walden.*

Consequently, in America and in many other countries, we have people who are physically strong but weak-willed. We have children using superior technology but receiving an inferior education. We have laws that are legally right but morally wrong. We have abundant food but less nutritional value in it. We have rich homes but relationally-poor families. We have greater quantity but lesser quality. We have more possessions but less contentment. These troubling conditions tell us that we urgently need the influence of wisdom in our lives, our families, our communities, our schools, our businesses, our governing bodies, and our nations.

WISDOM IS FOR EVERYONE

How can we obtain the wisdom we need? The world is filled with wisdom for us to gather, and it is available to anyone and everyone; we just need to discover and apply it. Some information and knowledge is geared toward people in particular fields, but the whole range of wisdom is wide open for all to receive its benefits. The ability to access and gain wisdom transcends culture, socioeconomic status, age, race, vocation, and any other category. I guarantee that if you will seek, learn, and apply wisdom, it will change your life for the better.

WISDOM IS A RESOURCE THAT NEVER RUNS DRY.

And wisdom is a resource that never runs dry. It stays with us throughout our lives as a continuous gift. It keeps working for us even after our parents, grandparents, teachers, and others whose advice we cherished have moved away or passed on. Those who have given us wise instruction through the years—either personally or through books, electronic media, or other sources—have provided a wonderful legacy for us. And even if we haven't yet applied the wisdom they imparted, we can make a commitment to do so starting now—not only helping ourselves to grow and succeed but enabling us to leave our own legacy of wisdom for those who come after us.

THE WISDOM-DRIVEN LIFE

In *Power Principles*, I have included key wisdom principles that will guide you into the countless benefits of the wisdom-driven life. I draw a number of foundational truths from the book of Proverbs, a significant work in the genre of Wisdom Literature. This wisdom has been known since ancient times; it is tried-and-true, and it is even more relevant to us today than the latest technology. It is not my desire to be ethereal about wisdom but to give you practical wisdom strategies that I believe will enhance and transform your life.

In these pages are potent chapters on significant topics relating to wisdom for people in all walks of life, especially leaders and others in positions of influence. There are wisdom principles to give you a basis for decision-making, help you develop profitable habits, address relationship problems in a constructive way, encourage you to develop positive attitudes, show you how to protect yourself from unnecessary pain and failure, help you establish new priorities, enable you to stabilize and grow your finances, and show you how to increase the value of what you contribute to others. You can build on these principles as you relate them to your own experiences and circumstances.

You may be interested in how to apply wisdom to your career or business. You are doing well, but you want to achieve even more. *Power Principles* will take you to that higher level. Or perhaps your success in business hasn't been matched by success in your family life or with a work/life balance. You will learn principles that will lead you to healthy living and personal satisfaction. Maybe you currently find yourself in a difficult situation; you have made certain decisions without thinking through the consequences, and now you need real wisdom because nothing seems to be working. You'll learn truths to help you get back on track.

We all need a wisdom perspective. Our outlook—how we perceive reality—really does determine our outcome. What you think about is usually what you will manifest. So let me ask you, "What's on your mind today?" Is it moving you in a positive direction or a negative one? The wisdom-driven perspective leads us to a life that is the most:

- ✦ fulfilling

- ✦ contented

- ✦ productive

- ✦ generous

It also enables us to avoid the greatest:

- ✦ mistakes

- ✦ regrets

- ✦ failures

- ✦ loss to ourselves and others

Wisdom holds everything together.

SEEDS OF WISDOM

I offer these power principles as seeds that can grow and flourish as you receive them and put them into practice. We cannot just appreciate wisdom insights or admire the wisdom of other people; we also need to discover and internalize a wise approach to life for ourselves. I encourage you to use this book to assess what is currently guiding your own life, to evaluate to what extent you are basing your life on wisdom principles—whether you are actually putting those principles into practice—and to reorder your life according to them. If you don't take the time to apply wisdom, then wisdom is really no good to you at all. Wisdom is not just a *knowing* but a *doing*. It not only gives us a framework for our lives, but it also helps us to understand what we need to do and how to implement it.

In the natural world, if you plant a seed in rich soil, that seed has a better chance to grow into a healthy and thriving plant. No matter how high-quality a seed might be, its success has much to do with the environment it is in. Similarly, when you plant a seed of wisdom into your circumstances, you want your life to be "good ground." In the physical world, after seeds are planted, they sprout up, pushing their way through the soil to flourish as plants and bring their benefits to the world, such as oxygen to breathe, fruit to eat, and beauty to enjoy. In the same way, wisdom will produce many beneficial things in your life if you give it good soil to germinate in.

Ultimately, we determine what kind of ground we are going to be. Perhaps you have received some good seeds of wisdom in the past, and you feel you should have been producing some fruit by now, but you are still dealing with the same frustrating issues and problems. It may be that you need to prepare your life as good ground by being open to receiving wisdom and then applying it one step at a time.

WE MUST DISCOVER AND INTERNALIZE A WISE APPROACH TO LIFE FOR OURSELVES.

Once you internalize any wisdom principle and act on it, you will eventually bear wisdom fruit in relation to it. But let me emphasize that no tree bears fruit to feed itself. Trees don't eat their own fruit; they bear fruit that nourishes human beings. In a similar way, the fruit we bear when we live according to wisdom is not for our own sake alone but for others who are in need of it and who will receive its benefits. You have wisdom about a particular issue that another person who is struggling with that issue does not have. Conversely, the fruit you need for the nourishment of your body, soul, or spirit will often come from someone else.

I encourage you to receive wisdom to nourish your own life, and then to bear wisdom fruit for others. We are meant to have a constant flow and exchange of wisdom with those around us. I have written this book as a contribution to that exchange, offering the wisdom fruit I have reaped from four decades of planting, nurturing, and harvesting wisdom principles. Because a strong legacy of wisdom has made a tremendous difference in my life, it is my desire to pass along these wisdom principles to those living in today's complex world and to future generations.

I have heard that some Asian families will teach their children tidbits of wisdom and then follow up by giving them a spoonful of honey. In this way, they create the connotation that wisdom is desirable and beneficial. It encourages the children to internalize the wisdom and to continue to pursue it. Let us likewise recognize the value of wisdom and seek to internalize wisdom principles for the lifelong pursuit and application of the wisdom-driven life.

RECEIVE WISDOM TO NOURISH YOUR LIFE AND THEN TO BEAR WISDOM FRUIT FOR OTHERS.

PART 1
THE WISDOM-DRIVEN LIFE

1

WISDOM IS THE PRINCIPAL THING

"Wisdom is the principal thing; therefore get wisdom.
And in all your getting, get understanding."[2]

A *Forbes* magazine columnist wrote an article entitled, "The Top 8 Things People Desperately Desire but Can't Seem to Attain," based on the responses from a survey of her subscribers and community. Those eight things were: (1) happiness, (2) money, (3) freedom, (4) peace, (5) joy, (6) balance, (7) fulfillment, and (8) confidence.[3]

We all wish for things to make our lives more satisfying and prosperous. Sometimes, attaining those desires can be elusive. That was certainly the case for those who participated in the above survey. But what if you were given the opportunity to have whatever you wished in life? What would you ask for?

---

2. Proverbs 4:7.
3. Kathy Caprino, "The Top 8 Things People Desperately Desire but Can't Seem to Attain," *Forbes*, May 24, 2016.

A newly crowned king in ancient times was given that very opportunity by God. You would think he might have asked for long life, honor, riches, or the destruction of his enemies. That would have been the conventional thinking about how a new monarch could immediately solidify and expand his reign. But instead, he asked for something that would enable him to obtain everything else he would need in life. One version of this story says he asked for "wisdom and knowledge."[4] The other says he asked for "an understanding heart,"[5] or "a discerning heart."[6] These are the same request in slightly different expressions.

This king's chief desire was to have the ability to govern his people judiciously. He needed to be able to distinguish right from wrong and good from evil, even in circumstances when it was difficult to tell which was which. For that, he needed *wisdom*. Everything else would take care of itself.

Because of this humble response, the king was granted not only wisdom but also wealth and renown. But it was a heart for wisdom that led him to that place.

That young ruler's name was King Solomon—the wisest man who ever lived.

What prompted Solomon, at the height of his newfound power, to ask for wisdom and discernment? Solomon had internalized the compelling advice that his father, King David, had taught him since he was a child:

Get wisdom! Get understanding!... Wisdom is the principal thing; therefore get wisdom. And in all your getting, get understanding. Exalt her, and she will promote you; she will bring you honor, when you embrace her.[7]

In essence, Solomon asked for the ability to discern himself, other people, and the world around him, so he could make the best decisions, plans, and strategies in life. A longing for wisdom filled his thinking and

---

4. 2 Chronicles 1:10.
5. 1 Kings 3:9.
6. 1 Kings 3:9 (NIV).
7. Proverbs 4:5, 7–8.

influenced his lifestyle. This is what all of us need. Everything else will be taken care of if we prioritize this "principal thing."

OUR MOST IMPORTANT RESOURCE

Solomon's answer to the momentous question presented to him reminds me of the lists of "top traits" found in many books and articles on leadership. Here is a list of some of those traits:

Results-oriented	Inspires others
Visionary	Team player
Has a clear strategy	Practices discipline
Delegates	Prioritizes
Resolves conflicts	Develops staff
Decisive	Confident
Trustworthy	Committed
Honest	Creative
Communicates well	Cultivates skills
Accountable	Innovates
Optimist	Able to adapt and change

These are all significant characteristics. But for leaders and people in all realms of life, "exercises wisdom" is the greatest trait. Wisdom is better than money, power, skill, facts, knowledge, vision, or physical assets because it is a wellspring of guidance and answers. Often, a wisdom principle doesn't just give us one answer to one question but can be applied in many contexts.

It has been said that the primary difference between "winners" and "losers" is their perspective. The best chance for true success in any arena or realm—whether business, government, community, nonprofit, education, church, family, or personal life—is to develop a perspective that will enhance, expand upon, and take us beyond what we already bring to the table. That unique outlook is a wisdom-driven perspective. *Power Principles* was written to highlight this key to personal, relational, and professional success that is so often overlooked today. A wisdom-driven perspective gives us the ability to deal astutely in the affairs of life and to achieve the success God intends for us to have.

YOUR OUTLOOK DETERMINES YOUR OUTCOME.

WISDOM SUBSTITUTES

Most people think of wisdom (if they think about it much at all) as the equivalent of knowledge. Others think of it as an aspect of their emotions or intuition, or as a kind of "sixth sense" about how to conduct their lives. Because of these mind-sets, they use their knowledge and emotions as substitutes for wisdom rather than as complements to it, not realizing that they are hindering their potential, effectiveness, and fulfillment in life.

SUBSTITUTING KNOWLEDGE FOR WISDOM

A man in Boston was hosting a friend who was a Chinese scholar and philosopher. He met this friend at the train station and then rushed him over to the subway. As they ran through the subway station, the man panted to his guest, "If we run…and catch the next train…we could save three minutes…." The Chinese philosopher replied, "And what significant things shall we do with the three minutes that we are saving?"

In many ways, we constantly seem to be trying to save ourselves "three minutes" in an attempt to radically improve our lives. And knowing that we have a mass of information and knowledge at the click of a computer mouse or the touch of a smart phone makes us feel secure that we can find the answers we seek and the keys for living better. Yet knowledge is simply facts and information, while wisdom is knowing the best thing to do with the information we have. It is making the right application of our knowledge for the highest benefits and effectiveness. We can gather a myriad of facts and obtain as much information as we want, but these won't help us sort out the issues of life if we don't know the right thing to do or the next step to take.

Wisdom is often thought of as something ethereal and intangible. But what I appreciate most about wisdom is its *complete practicality*. Wisdom enables us to assimilate information, understand how various elements work in relation to one another, and put our knowledge into practice. *Wisdom* is an action word—it knows *what* to do, *when* to do it, and *how* to do it—and then it follows up and *does* it. Wisdom gets the job done.

WISDOM IS AN ACTION WORD—IT KNOWS *WHAT* TO DO, *WHEN* TO DO IT, AND *HOW* TO DO IT—AND THEN IT FOLLOWS UP AND *DOES* IT.

The majority of people seek knowledge without wisdom, and then they can't understand why they aren't doing well or why they can't move to the next stage of growth in their business, finances, or relationships. Only when we understand and apply the corresponding wisdom to our knowledge can we break free of frustrating cycles that have kept us spinning our wheels and move forward. Wisdom enables us to advance to new levels.

Many of us have questions such as:

+ How can I know my true purpose in life?
+ How can I be a better leader?
+ What is the next step for my business?
+ How can I help my organization to grow?
+ Should I be training for a different job or vocation?
+ How should I deal with this relationship problem?
+ How can I live a more balanced life?
+ How can I help my children prepare for an uncertain future?

These are all questions that require wisdom, not knowledge alone, to answer. This doesn't mean that information and knowledge aren't necessary, but they are just not enough. "Knowledge is power," the saying goes. Yet wisdom is the true power because, again, it tells us how to use the knowledge we have gained to the greatest effect.

SUBSTITUTING EMOTIONS FOR WISDOM

The second approach to living that many people follow is to function primarily according to their emotions rather than stepping back to discern the best course to take. In this case, knowledge, as well as wisdom, usually takes a backseat. Some people may be using wisdom in one area of their lives while being derailed by their emotions in other areas. Motivators like fear, guilt, and desire have a strong influence. Fear can make us procrastinate about pursuing a good opportunity. Unresolved guilt can cause us to feel unworthy of success or of healthy relationships. The thrilling prospect of a new business deal can lead us to rush into an association without first considering all the ramifications.

When we lose sight of the value of wisdom—or when we have never understood its worth—we overlook the primary source of principles for improving our lives, our families, our relationships, and our vocations. We miss out on a wealth of practical help for living, working, and interacting with others. Wisdom reveals to us a deeper picture of things. It enables us to have a life that is purposeful and satisfying as well as successful, utilizing the contributions of both our knowledge and our healthy emotions while keeping them in balance.

BUILDING KNOWLEDGE, UNDERSTANDING, AND WISDOM

When King David gave his advice to Solomon, he said, "Get wisdom. And in all your getting, get understanding." How do we "get wisdom" in order to apply it to our lives? To begin, we must recognize that knowledge, understanding, and wisdom are related as three sequential steps.

Step one is to gain knowledge. We accumulate facts and information.

Step two is to develop understanding. We assimilate the facts and perceive how various facts and information correspond to one another. To understand is to discern, to comprehend, and to interpret. Very few people intentionally take this step, so they remain at the knowledge level. But as we collect information, we should begin to integrate those bits of data and to consider their implications. Knowledge can help us to take things apart and understand them, but wisdom enables us to relate knowledge and truth to everyday life.

Step three is to live in wisdom. We put our knowledge and understanding into active use. As I described earlier, wisdom is knowing *what* to do, *when* to do it, and *how* to do it—and then following up and *doing* it; it is the ability to live life skillfully. A lot of people know what to do but they don't know how to do it. Wisdom involves the know-how. Wisdom is deeper than knowledge because wisdom is as wisdom does.

We need discernment in order to understand what life is truly about, combined with the motivation and discipline to live life wisely. For example, you may have talent but not be using it in the best way. You may have knowledge but not be applying it most effectively. You may have an idea with tremendous potential but not know how to develop it. You may have much love to give but be investing it in unhealthy relationships. Wisdom— the combination of knowledge, understanding, and action—produces a strategy, and a strategy produces success.

WISDOM PRODUCES A STRATEGY,
AND A STRATEGY PRODUCES SUCCESS.

WHAT ARE YOU BASING YOUR LIFE ON?

Few people today are asking the question, "Am I living my life according to wisdom?" If presented with the same offer Solomon was given, they would not request wisdom because they do not recognize its supreme value. We make so many unnecessary mistakes and create so many problems for ourselves by not stopping to consider what would be the wisest choice or the most astute course of action—for our present circumstances and for the future. Think of some of the mistakes you have made in the past. Don't you wish you had known better at the time—or had acted upon the better way that you knew? By learning and applying wisdom principles and by developing a lifestyle of pursuing wisdom, we can avoid many errors and missteps.

Could it be that you have been trying to sustain yourself on information or emotions alone? You may have never considered the vital role of wisdom in your life before now. Or perhaps you already have a good understanding of wisdom principles—and had every good intention of living according to them—but you've been sidetracked because of the busyness, stresses, and distractions of life. It's easier to live on autopilot than to stop to consider what is really directing our lives, especially when we don't get much reinforcement in wise living from the world around us. The general attitude in our society is to look for quick fixes—not necessarily the best, the strongest, or the most long-lasting solutions. But wisdom is like a weight-bearing beam in a house. You can't remove it or weaken it without jeopardizing the entire structure. In *Power Principles: The Benefits of a Wisdom-Driven Life*, you'll learn how to establish wisdom as a solid framework for your life as we explore how...

- Wisdom shows us the best way to live.
- Wisdom helps us to know the next step to take.
- Wisdom brings peace, perspective, and new opportunities.
- Wisdom can be applied to every realm of our lives.
- Wisdom is not only to be received for ourselves but is also to be shared with others.

Wisdom is like a trusted counselor—guiding us to make the best decisions, cautioning us against mistakes and failures, and enabling us to review our progress and to make good plans for the future.

Let's follow King David's advice: "Get wisdom! Get understanding!" Let wisdom be your most important resource. Let wisdom be your foundation and framework for living. Let wisdom show you the best way to respond in each situation and guide you throughout your life.

It is *the principal thing.*

BENEFITS OF A WISDOM-DRIVEN LIFE

- ◆ Wisdom gives us the ability to deal astutely in the affairs of life.
- ◆ Wisdom makes the best application of our knowledge and information.
- ◆ Wisdom enables us to avoid mistakes and mishaps.
- ◆ Wisdom produces a strategy, and a strategy produces success.

APPLYING WISDOM

1. What is the best advice you were ever given? Why do you consider it the best?

2. Did you follow through and apply this advice? Why or why not? If so, what difference did it make in your life?

3. What is the "principal thing" in your life today? Does it support or detract from living according to wisdom?

2

WISDOM LEADS US TO OUR PURPOSE

A career is what you're paid for,
but a calling is what you're made for.

I have stated that wisdom shows us what to do, when to do it, and how to do it. The next principle is that this know-how is directly connected to fulfilling our purpose in life. Those whose lives are guided by wisdom have as one of their top goals discerning their purpose and enthusiastically pursuing it. The reason many people are unsuccessful—or find it difficult to get to higher levels of success—is that they are not aware of their true purpose. Or, if they are aware of it, they're not following it.

DISCOVERING YOUR TRUE PURPOSE

YOUR DOMINANT GIFT

How do you discover—or confirm—your true purpose? Our purpose is closely linked to our *dominant gift*. Amid the hurried pace of life, it's often easy to forget that our gifts are different from our skills. A gift is inborn, something that is natural to us and is linked to our makeup as a person. A skill is something we have learned through hands-on experience, whether or not it aligns well with our natural gifts.

Solomon wrote, "A [person's] gift makes room for him, and brings him before great men."[8] I don't think it's an accident that Solomon used the word "gift" in the singular. Each of us has a unique gift that will ultimately bring us success. It is where our strength lies. This dominant gift is the key to our prosperity; it can impact our lives not only financially but also mentally, emotionally, and spiritually. Our primary gift might be a keen business sense, academic ability, or a creative capacity such as writing, painting, or singing. It might be athletic talent, scientific aptitude, or a knack for organizing people or events. It might be the ability to show compassion to others in tangible ways or to know how best to serve people in a specific area of need.

Your dominant gift is what gives you a distinct place in this world and a singular way to contribute to it. You'd be surprised what doors can open for you when you offer your God-given gift to others. When you discover your gift and pursue it, the world will respond and make room for you in ways you may never have imagined.

YOUR DOMINANT GIFT IS
THE KEY TO YOUR PROSPERITY.

You may be actively using your dominant gift, or you may be uncertain of what that gift is. You may be the CEO of a large corporation with years of professional experience, or you may be a college student just starting out. No matter what your situation, it's essential to recognize your dominant gift and how to apply it to truly make the most of your life and fulfill your potential.

---

8. Proverbs 18:16.

Perhaps you keep looking for business opportunities or financial schemes to try to figure out what will make you the most money so you can eventually do what you *really* want to do. That rarely helps. Instead, you need to focus on your dominant gift. Then you can seek financial opportunities that will help you apply the gift God has placed in your life.

There's nothing wrong with making money; in fact, some people's dominant gift is the ability to generate finances and raise funds. However, I have often seen people diverge from their purpose in order to focus exclusively on making money, only to experience personal decline. There is a deterioration of their enthusiasm for life, of their love for their spouse and children, and even of their character. It isn't a sudden drop but rather happens over time. For example, some people are fooled into thinking they can never make it as a successful, *honest* businessperson, so they start doing things that are unethical in order to get ahead. But when people allow wrong voices and wrong motivations to influence them, pain and failure enter their lives in various forms.

Note that if we have given access in our lives to people who are a negative influence, they do not usually leave voluntarily. We have to put them out of our lives. The only time a wrong influence may leave voluntarily is if we become broke. Then they don't need us anymore.

If we turn the wrong way by diverging from our purpose, our life will begin to go downward. If we turn the right way according to our purpose, our life will begin to ascend. Either way, there is a turning of the mind, the will, the emotions, the imagination, and the heart. We can avoid downturns in our life by maintaining the pursuit of our true purpose and gifting.

PRIMARY GIFTING AND MULTIPLE GIFTS

Most people have more than one gift, and some people are gifted in a variety of ways. That is why multi-gifted or multi-talented individuals often have a harder time identifying their dominant gift. While we often need to employ secondary gifts while fulfilling our main gift, the primary gift still leads the others. Therefore, even if you are able to do a lot of things, learn to recognize your primary area of gifting. It's possible that your dominant gift is lying dormant, and the gift you are chiefly using now is actually secondary.

HOW TO IDENTIFY YOUR DOMINANT GIFT

DESIGN, POTENTIAL, AND CALLING

Your purpose in life reflects your design and potential as an individual. Think about your natural abilities, talents, and desires. Then ask yourself, "What brings me the greatest fulfillment and personal satisfaction?" Follow up with this crucial question: "How do I want to be remembered?" Your answers to these questions will often reveal your purpose and gifting—and wisdom will guide you in activating them.

Let me repeat the saying found at the beginning of this chapter: "A career is what you're *paid* for, but a calling is what you're *made* for" (while also providing financial resources). The word *vocation* comes from the word *vocare*, meaning "to call." So a vocation is *a state of calling*, not just a career choice. Understanding purpose enables us to step into the calling we were made for.

When people don't know what they want, it is a problem of insufficient knowledge. When people don't pursue what they want, it is a problem of motivation. When people don't achieve what they want, it is often a problem of persistence. All three of these issues can be addressed once we discover our dominant gift.

Moreover, when we learn our purpose, it becomes the primary way in which we measure our success or failure in life. We can't do everything, but we can do everything that God intends for us to do, everything that is related to our purpose.

IT'S WHO YOU ARE

To identify our dominant gift, we should also recognize that our gift is not fundamentally what we do; in a sense, it is who we are—we are the gift, because it comes from within us. Of course, we are not our gift in a direct sense, but we and our gift are interconnected in such a way that the two cannot be separated.

Neither is our gift something we own. Thus, the gift that makes room for you is not what you possess—rather, it's what "possesses" you. You don't merely have it; it has you. Let me emphasize that it is not someone else's idea of what would be good for you to do or pursue in life. As we will see, other people can assist us in identifying our gift, but ultimately, we have to affirm it. Ask yourself, "Is what I am currently doing with my life what I really want to do? Does it reflect who I truly am? Does it fit my personality?" It takes a certain kind of personality to be a salesperson, or a counselor, or an accountant, or a physician, or a government official, or a company president, or any other vocation or role. When you tap into your purpose and recognize what God has placed inside you, then you will begin to discover your true calling. In this sense, your purpose is not something you choose; it's something you discover was within you all along.

THE GIFT THAT MAKES ROOM FOR YOU IS NOT WHAT YOU POSSESS—IT'S WHAT "POSSESSES" YOU.

IT'S WHAT MAKES YOU COME ALIVE INSIDE

Because your gift is an expression of who you are, when you exercise that gift, it makes you come alive; it makes you *feel* alive. Perhaps your career is doing something good and useful, but it's not something that makes you feel alive. You accepted the job because it's a safe position and has benefits. Too many people go to school just to get trained to work in a career or vocation that is not suited to them. When they do this, they get bent out of shape just trying to fit in. If people are working in a situation where they don't want to be, you can usually tell by their sad expression or negative attitude. But those who are following their calling have a clear vision that fills them with excitement.

I love to talk with visionary people because it energizes me. Enthusiasm comes from the heart; it is not something you put on but something that you release. When you find the thing that makes you come alive, power will come into your life. So find what you love to do and do it enthusiastically!

What makes you come alive? Is it when you are drawing up a business plan, meeting someone's health needs, designing buildings, or running a race? My wife's unique calling is in music. She tells me that her life would be very bland without music—it would be like living in a world with only gray tones and no color. There are many people whose dominant gift is a musical talent, and they are out singing or playing an instrument wherever and whenever they can. Even though they are making financial sacrifices in order to do it, they wouldn't do anything else because the gift comes from within them.

Music is not my dominant gift, so a life without music wouldn't really bother me much. Instead, I come alive when I teach and mentor people in leadership. We all have something that causes life to be in full color for us. If you will just do what makes you come alive, the world will indeed be a blessed place! The world benefits from people who have come alive in their purpose, not those who don't even realize why they are here. There are too many frustrated people living unsatisfied lives in a career that they're paid for, instead of finding their calling, which they're made for.

Some people spend lots of time researching what jobs and fields are hiring right now, and that approach can be helpful in finding our place of contribution to the world. Yet if you are frustrated in your workplace or searching for a new job, ask yourself, "What would I do even if I were not paid to do it?" The answer to this question can point you directly toward your dominant gift. You can be secure in who you were created to be and in the dominant gift you have been given. You don't have to try to run anybody else's race.

IT'S WHAT YOU ARE PASSIONATE ABOUT

You know you are using your dominant gift when you are genuinely passionate about what you are doing. What is it that possesses you to the degree that it wakes you up in the middle of the night and urges you to get up and work on it—where ideas start coming to your mind and you begin planning, designing, or writing? What interrupts your thought patterns in the middle of the day, so that you start thinking about how you can expand something or make it better or stronger? What do you see in your mind's eye even when you're looking at something else? What do you hear "speaking" to you even when you're conversing with other people? This is your gift saying, "Give me a way to express myself!"

Make a list of the things that you love to do or wish you could do, things that you know you would do every day with joy. Include any ideas that you just can't let go of, things that are deep down inside you and always seem to surface in your thoughts. What do these things have in common? How might they point to your dominant gift?

Once that list is made, begin to see the possibilities of applying your gift. Do some research on the Internet and elsewhere. Talk to friends and relatives and neighbors. Seek out somebody who is working in the same field and ask them about their work and their life. Get input from all of these resources to help you discover what you're really made for.

As you research, see if there's an opening or opportunity in the area you are passionate about. Some people begin to pursue their dream by doing an internship or taking on a part-time job or a volunteer position in their field of interest. Don't allow pride to keep you from starting small and working toward what you ultimately want.

What good will it do to wear yourself out working sixty, seventy, eighty hours a week in a job that you hate in order to earn money, if you're miserable and unfulfilled? You may have a lot of money with which you can buy material things; but the more stuff you get, the less satisfied you will be inside. Again, true fulfillment results from living out your purpose, and this comes from understanding and using your gift. You might end up working many hours a week using your dominant gift, but you will be energized by it, not drained by it, because you will have found your purpose in life.

You don't want to reach a point where you say to yourself, *There's got to be more to life than this. I don't know how I'm going to keep up this kind of existence.* Your gift may or may not bring in the kind of money you originally thought you would be making or that your relatives thought you should be earning. Or, it might bring you much more financially than you imagined. Either way, using your gift will bring greater satisfaction, peace, and contentment to your life.

DON'T ALLOW PRIDE TO KEEP YOU FROM STARTING SMALL AND WORKING TOWARD WHAT YOU ULTIMATELY WANT.

IT'S STRONGER THAN OBSTACLES THAT COME AGAINST IT

When you understand your purpose, you develop a passion to fulfill it, and that passion makes you resilient and able to spring back from the challenges life dishes out to you. Passion is a source of real determination and gives us the ability to overcome resistance and other difficulties as we operate in our calling.

Passion and resilience fuel us to the point that we are willing to accept temporary discomfort and setbacks for long-term gain. If you are passionate about your gift, and you experience a setback, you don't say, "Well, I guess I'm washed up in this particular area." In fact, it is often the case that we are challenged in the very area of our gifting. If we expect this, we can be ready for the obstacles that come and threaten to derail the pursuit of our purpose. If you are still following your purpose after people have tried to discourage you, and after circumstances have almost overwhelmed you, you know you were meant for it.

IT REQUIRES THE HELP OF OTHERS

It's rare that anyone exercises their dominant gift in isolation or doesn't need the cooperation of others to fulfill their purpose. In fact, if we can go it alone, our vision isn't big enough. Often, the full implementation of our purpose will involve other gifts or skills that we don't have or can't learn to do with proficiency. We need to master our dominant gift while teaming up with those who have primary gifts that can supplement or complement ours. For example, someone with the gift of manufacturing products needs to work with a distributor to get their products into the marketplace. Someone with the gift of writing screenplays won't see their script become a film until it is produced by a studio or a production company that employs people with a variety of other creative and technical gifts. Purpose and teamwork go together.

CLARIFYING YOUR DOMINANT GIFT

The following are some helpful ways you can clarify your dominant gift and work through any uncertainty you may have in identifying it. I have incorporated some of the ideas we discussed above. Each of these ways is useful, and they are not listed in a particular order of importance.

TRIAL AND ERROR

All of us have tried something and realized, "I am not cut out for this. This is just not me." It may be an activity you participated in once, or it may be a job you struggled with for years before you finally admitted it was not a good fit. You know from trial and error that it's not right for you because it didn't use your main gifting or fill you with excitement and energy.

It would be unwise for us to try to pursue one of our lesser gifts or to use a skill in which we are weak as if it were our dominant gift. However, remember that as we exercise our primary gift, we may have to perform secondary tasks related to it that we don't particularly like doing or don't feel entirely skilled at, even though we are able to perform them. Sometimes that goes with the territory as we pursue the big picture of fulfilling our purpose. But let me add this: *You may leave your comfort zone, but don't ever leave your gift zone.* Even though you sometimes have to perform those other activities, make sure your focus remains on your dominant gift and vision.

THE PERSPECTIVES OF OTHERS

A second way to get an understanding of your dominant gift is through the perspectives of other people who can give you feedback about your strengths and weaknesses. Talk to people who will tell you the truth about yourself and not just tell you what they think you want to hear. Sometimes your best mirror is the collective opinions of your friends and family who really know you, because those who know you best can often see things in you that you can't see in yourself. A friend or sibling may say to you, "Why are you doing that job? You ought to be doing such and such. You're so good at it." You may not have recognized a certain ability or a volunteer activity as being related to your dominant gift. You've been treating it as an avocation, while other people have already recognized it as a viable vocation for you.

Just one word of caution: consider carefully what other people say, but make sure their advice resonates with you. As we discussed earlier, other people's opinions and suggestions are sometimes based on factors outside your dominant gift. For example, they may want you to follow in the footsteps of a relative who worked in a certain field, even though that field doesn't align with your primary gifting. Nevertheless, people close to you can often be very helpful in identifying your dominant gift.

PERSONALITY TESTS

There are various questionnaires available online or in printed form that can help you identify your personality type; what you enjoy doing most, and in what settings you enjoy doing it; what gifts you have; and which of your gifts is most prominent. Such tests can help you to recognize a gift you have been using successfully and happily in another context but hadn't thought about in terms of a calling.

REWARDING EXPERIENCES

Another way to discern your dominant gift is to reflect on activities and events you have been involved with throughout your life that have been the most rewarding and satisfying to you. Think through your various personal experiences and ask yourself these questions: "What type of activity, endeavor, or work has been consistently gratifying to me?" "What was I doing at a time in my life when I felt the most fulfilled?" "What have I done that has brought great joy to me?"

Often, the most satisfying experiences will center on a particular gift or trait. When making your assessment, be sure to think back to when you were younger and probably had more time and freedom to enjoy favorite activities. Additionally, many people will make time for the things that are most fulfilling to them. Therefore, what you make time for, even when your schedule is full, can reveal your dominant gift.

FAMILY ROOTS

For certain people, studying their ancestry can give them a clue to their primary gift. Sometimes you don't know what you are capable of until you discover what some of your forebears were able to do. Of course, you might discover some things in your ancestry that you're not proud of! On the other hand, you might come across some unique abilities and giftings your ancestors and relatives had that you have, as well, because you share their DNA.

INSPIRATION

I believe in the power of prayer for wisdom and guidance. I encourage you to ask the Creator to reveal what He put inside you that He wants you to share with the world. Again, you may be surprised to find that your gift or vision is bigger than you think. Our own vision can be greatly limited. But when we make a connection with the Creator and ask Him to reveal His plans, the results are often greater than we could have imagined.

STIR UP YOUR GIFT

Once you discover your dominant gift, it needs to be stirred up within you so it can be manifested. Again, a good way to do this is to spend time with people who have a similar gift and watch how they exercise it. Have you ever been around somebody who has a gift similar to yours, and you suddenly became excited about new possibilities? The exposure to the other person has helped to stir up your own gift and motivated you to exercise it.

You also stir up your gift by taking it seriously, thinking about its potential, and making specific plans to implement it, rather than just hoping you can use it someday. Pablo Picasso said, "I paint objects as I think them, not as I see them." His paintings were expressions of his thoughts. If you don't begin to consistently think about exercising your gift, you'll never see it become a full reality. But when you start thinking about it and stirring it up, you can demonstrate to the world what you've already envisioned internally.

ACT ON YOUR GIFT

The more you stir up your dominant gift, the more it will flow out of your life. We shouldn't assume that our gift is functioning at its maximum capacity just because it's inherent. Though a primary gift is inborn, it can and should be developed throughout our lives.

Most people fail because they fail to execute. Don't be afraid to step out and use your primary gift in a definite way in relation to your purpose—whether you have an idea for an original product, a plan for new business, a concept for a book, an innovative way to market a service, a program to serve your community, or anything else.

Our gift won't mean anything unless it is used. Even if you're not currently in a position where you have the freedom to do all that is in your heart, hold on to your dream of giving your gift to the world and continually prepare yourself for opportunities to share it.

Relatedly, a gift is not a gift until it is *given*. If you never share your particular gift, using it for the benefit of other people, you haven't really understood its purpose. Earlier, I wrote about how Solomon asked God for a discerning heart. The wisdom he was asking for was not for himself but so that he could accurately discern his people's situations and judge them justly. Ultimately, our gifts are for the purpose of serving others.

"YOU ARE THE ONLY PERSON ON EARTH
WHO CAN USE YOUR ABILITY."
—ZIG ZIGLAR

CONTINUE TO USE AND SHARPEN YOUR GIFT

Even after you have exercised your gift successfully, don't neglect it. You haven't reached your highest point yet. Your dominant ability is a gift that keeps on giving. Just when you think you can't go any further with it, another facet of it will come bubbling up, and your gift will suddenly become stirred up again with new ideas and fresh applications.

If you don't regularly stir up your gift, it may begin to diminish and become less effective. You might even lose sight of it altogether through disuse. But your gift will increase and grow stronger as you continue to exercise it, develop it, and innovate with it.

Whatever your circumstances, you should be dreaming of where you want to go in life; wisdom will help you to reach that dream as you pursue your purpose. You don't want to be stuck in the best that you have already done. You want to move forward to the best that you can do. Don't focus on your history but rather on your potential. What you see in your imagination, as well as the thoughts that dominate your mind, will always rule your world.

"IF YOU THINK YOU ARE TOO SMALL TO MAKE A DIFFERENCE, TRY SLEEPING WITH A MOSQUITO."
—ATTRIBUTED TO DALAI LAMA XIV

BENEFITS OF A WISDOM-DRIVEN LIFE

+ Wisdom helps us to discern our purpose and pursue its fulfillment through our dominant gift.

+ Our dominant gift is the key to our prosperity. It gives us a distinct place in the world and a singular way to contribute to others.

+ When we know our purpose, we have the true measure of success or failure in life.

+ We can strengthen and improve our dominant gift by understanding it, focusing on it, and using it.

APPLYING WISDOM

+ Help clarify your purpose in life by taking time to answer the question, "How would I like to be remembered?" Write down your thoughts.

+ Discover or confirm your dominant gift by reviewing the section "Clarifying Your Dominant Gift" and by asking yourself the various questions posed in this chapter, such as:

  › Is what I am currently doing with my life what I really want to do?

  › Does it reflect who I truly am? Does it fit my personality?

  › What activities and talents make me feel the most alive when I participate in them or use them?

  › What ideas for doing or creating something persistently surface in my thoughts?

  As you answer these questions, make a list of things that you love to do, wish you could do, and know you would do every day with joy.

+ Once you begin identifying your purpose and primary gift, start researching and planning how you will pursue your purpose while developing your gift.

3

WISDOM TRUSTS THE JOURNEY

Wisdom is a journey, not a destination.

We need to think of wisdom as a journey, not as a place we arrive at and are suddenly wise. We never stop learning wisdom but continue to collect it through the years to apply to our lives. In a parallel way, as we discover or confirm our purpose in life, we should realize that although we can know our purpose, we won't know the full story of our calling until we live it out. God will unfold facets of our purpose along life's journey, so we have to travel the journey in order for that purpose to be completely revealed.

As we proceed along the wisdom journey, we will receive everything we need to fulfill our calling. And though we don't always know where we're headed, wisdom trusts the journey to take us there. Genuine trust surfaces in our lives and becomes significant to our progress in life only in times of uncertainty or ambiguity. We step out into our purpose by faith, without knowing the full picture. We put one foot in front of the other and leave our comfortable place to launch out to do something of which we don't have any concrete guarantees.

You might never have thought you would have the boldness to move forward with intention and passion, prompted by the gift and calling God has placed in your heart. But something happens when you commit to your purpose that starts a momentum in your life, sending you on a new course to greater fulfillment and success. Let's explore some specific benefits of a life journey guided by wisdom and purpose.

BENEFITS OF THE JOURNEY

1. THE JOURNEY INTRODUCES US TO OURSELVES

First, there's something about the journey that helps to introduce us to ourselves and to make wisdom real to us. We will have experiences along our journey that may seem unlikely aids in fulfilling our calling, but they are all part of the process and preparation for it. In this way, the journey not only teaches us wisdom but also enables us to internalize it, establishing it in our lives so that we consistently live by its principles.

Long ago, a young man became the equivalent of prime minister of Egypt seemingly overnight, but his journey to that position was long and unlikely. He was first sold into slavery by his own brothers. But his innate gifts and abilities caused him to be promoted to the position of his master's most trusted servant—until he was falsely accused and sent to prison. Yet even in prison, he didn't languish over the injustices he suffered but continued to exercise his gifts where he was. As a result, the jailor appointed him to be his top prison administrator. All this time, even under trying circumstances, the young man's gift was being stirred up and developed, waiting for the right opportunity to flourish.

One day, the pharaoh had a problem that only this man's unique purpose and abilities could answer, and the young man suddenly went from being a prisoner to being the second highest ruler in Egypt. But he never could have fulfilled the administrative duties of a prime minister if he hadn't been exercising his gifts all along.[9]

The same principle applies to us. We cannot afford to wait until we get to a certain place in life before we decide to exercise our abilities and

9. For the full account, see Genesis 37, 39–41.

potential. We have to be faithful to continually develop them and to keep gaining wisdom, even if we're in a place of obscurity and think nobody notices us or appreciates what we can do.

We want to be able to fully live all the days we have on this earth. We don't want come to the end of our life regretting the things that we failed to do—things that we could have…would have…should have done. As someone wisely said, the greatest tragedy in life is not to die but rather to have never lived.

That's why you shouldn't let anybody else put your life on hold. You can't wait on anybody else for you to start living; you just have to move forward and let them catch up with you. You are placed on this earth to thrive, not merely to survive. You are here to live life to the maximum and have no regrets when you pass on. It's not how long you live but what you give while you are here that matters.

THE JOURNEY NOT ONLY TEACHES US WISDOM BUT ALSO ENABLES US TO INTERNALIZE IT.

Let me say to those at the beginning of their life's journey: you don't often step directly into your calling after you graduate from high school or college. Sometimes you have to do what you have to do until you can do what you were called to do. You need certain experiences to prepare you for what is coming. You will enter into and fulfill your purpose as long as you make this commitment in your heart: "I'm going to live my calling—no matter how much I have to go the extra mile, no matter what other people say, and regardless of how much I have to work with every ounce of my being."

Before I entered my main vocation, I delivered newspapers, was a cashier in a drugstore, and worked as an accountant and a salesman. I even had a job working in a health food store, cutting cheese and wrapping it. God sometimes leads us in roundabout ways to cause us to end up where we're designed to be. You may not know why you have to go through what you go through, but it's all part of the journey to your purpose.

Wherever you are in life, I encourage you to start demonstrating whatever God has placed inside you. New and greater opportunities will come if you are already busy at your purpose—working on something, creating something, building something. Wisdom knows that the person who is faithful in that which is least is also faithful in that which is much.[10]

2. THE JOURNEY AIDS OUR PERSONAL DEVELOPMENT

The journey also has a significant role in our personal development, in helping us become who we were meant to be. We have to receive the wisdom and the beauty of the journey; the path contains both adversity and joy, but we should learn to appreciate both (hard as that may be at times), because each plays a significant part: one is for growth and the other for blessing.

It's not really about what you do in life; it's about what you become in the process of what you do. Some people are so focused on the destination that they miss the benefits of the journey. We need to set goals and know what we are aiming for in life, but again, we must also experience the process. And the process will teach us wisdom and build good character in us if we allow it to. God's purpose in your life is greater than your problems, your pain, your obstacles, and your mistakes. He doesn't disqualify you when you go through difficulties or mess up; His purposes will still be fulfilled.

IT'S NOT REALLY ABOUT WHAT YOU DO IN LIFE BUT
ABOUT WHAT YOU BECOME IN THE PROCESS.

3. THE JOURNEY BRINGS PEOPLE INTO OUR LIVES WHO CAN HELP US

Additionally, you will encounter various people along the way who will be able to assist you in your life journey. You won't meet some people until

10. See Luke 16:10.

you get to a fork in the road, and then they'll be there to give you the guidance to choose the right path, the resources to move forward with your
purpose, or anything else you may need. If you diverge from your purpose
in an attempt to pursue something else, you will get off-track and may miss
these encounters.

I met my wife when I was in high school, but at the time, I wasn't looking for a girlfriend or a wife. I wasn't out trying to find women for its own
sake. Even at that age, I was following what I knew of my purpose, and I
was introduced to my wife along the way. In fact, when I first saw her, we
were in a high school hallway where the lockers were located; our lockers
were near one another, and she tripped over her friend's foot and literally
fell at my feet! I didn't have to go out of my way to find her—she stumbled
on my path, so I couldn't miss her.

Likewise, it is not a coincidence that you bump into the people you're
supposed to meet on your journey. You don't have to go out of your way to get
what's designed for you. This doesn't mean you might not change locations or
circumstances in life as you pursue your calling. But if you're following your
true purpose and are alert to opportunities, you won't have to worry or strive
to obtain what you need. The person who can help you at a given point in
your life might be somebody on your job, somebody in your neighborhood,
even somebody who shops at the same store you do. You will meet many
people in life whom you can learn from, connect with, or receive help from.

4. THE JOURNEY PREPARES US FOR OUR DESTINATION

Moreover, we could never be prepared for our destination, or the fulfillment of our purpose, without traveling the path of our particular journey. There are gifts and abilities that you won't discover in life until you encounter certain circumstances and situations. Sometimes you don't know
what you can do until you have to do it, and then you are surprised at what
is inside you. That's why a mother eagle will push her eaglets out of the nest
after she has nurtured them for a while. They don't know they can fly until
they have to.

There will be some situations in life where our trust will be put on
trial. Will we trust the journey? Will we trust the Creator who placed our

purpose inside us and gave us the gift that motivates us to continue the journey? We don't know all the details ahead of time, but that's okay because He goes with us. Sometimes He just wants to surprise us with some good things along the way. Other times, He knows it's better for us not to know or experience certain things until we're strong enough to handle the pressures or challenges we will face.

Accordingly, there are various things on the journey of this life that we won't understand until we get to a particular place called "there." Have you ever heard older people talk about something, but you couldn't really identify with what they were saying until you later experienced something like it? It's similar to how teenagers usually think they know more than their fathers and mothers, and they don't understand certain things about their parents until they get "there" and become parents themselves; then they look back and realize how wise their parents were.

Often, "there" is the place where we have an epiphany, the place where a revelation of wisdom, knowledge, or insight comes to us. "There" might be the place that becomes a defining moment in our life where something comes alive to us, where the gifts of God are released, where our passion is stirred because of something we have discovered on our journey. "There" is sometimes where we are called to the next major step in the fulfillment of our purpose. But in order to encounter "there," we have to start on our journey and get busy doing what we are meant to do.

Sometimes we can be grateful if we haven't been given the best opportunities or success earlier in life because, at the time, we wouldn't have had enough maturity to handle them, build on them, or sustain them. After we've experienced some of the journey and have gained wisdom, we can better use and enjoy what we have and what we receive. If I had to choose which half of my life I would like to be the best, I would prefer to struggle while I was young and then be served the "good wine" in the second half of life, rather than the other way around.

Sometimes we just need to wait until the timing is right. Or for our gift to mature. Or for strategic people to be in place who will recognize the value of our abilities and qualities. That is when our gift will make room for us in the world. It would be foolish for us to sow a seed one day and dig it up the next day and expect the seed to have done its work. Life happens by a process.

A mushroom can grow in six hours. You can go to bed at night, and in the morning, a mushroom will have popped up that you didn't even see the day before. But a mushroom can also wither under the heat of the sun in a matter of hours. If you get something very fast, it might not last. But something that comes by a process is built for longevity. A mosquito egg hatches within two days, and the whole lifespan of the adult mosquito is a week to a month. In contrast, an elephant goes through a gestational period of almost two years and the animal lives for decades. My question to you is: Do you want a mosquito blessing or an elephant blessing?

SOMETIMES YOU DON'T KNOW WHAT YOU CAN DO
UNTIL YOU HAVE TO DO IT.

THE BEST PATH

Some people delay starting their journey to purpose, saying, "I'm just waiting for inspiration to hit me," or "I'm waiting for the right job to come along," or "I'm waiting for something to happen." There's a place for patience and waiting, but that's not what they're doing. They're waiting for their ship to come in. Let me tell you: your ship is not going to come in—you have to swim out to meet it!

Remember that opportunity will bring you from one thing to something else—not from nothing to something. So do the things that God has placed in your heart. Follow your dream. Your steps will become more intentional and deliberate as you go along. Put yourself to use on the level where you currently are, being faithful and productive, while keeping alert and prepared for the next opportunity.

There's nothing more frustrating than not being ready for an opportunity when it arrives. However, let me encourage you that if you do miss an opportunity, don't give up—another one will come along. Wisdom will lead you to it on your journey. I don't necessarily agree with the adage "Opportunity never knocks twice." We may or may not have a second chance at a particular opportunity. But I believe in the God of possibilities and second chances. And that means that there will always be opportunities for us to work, to create, to serve, and to love.

Suppose you are running late and hurrying to catch a subway (similar to the host of the Chinese philosopher in the story from earlier in this book). You rush down the steps just as the train car closes its doors and pulls away. You missed that train—but another one will be coming along to pick up passengers in just a few minutes. It's already on the track; it's there, even though you can't see it physically. Often, you can hear the train coming before you can actually see it. So if you have already missed one chance, start preparing for the next one. Opportunities will come and go. You have to work to be ready to receive that next opportunity. And living according to wisdom will help you to do that, because wisdom always helps us discover and follow the best path for our life.

WISDOM HELPS US TO DISCOVER AND FOLLOW
THE BEST PATH FOR OUR LIFE.

BENEFITS OF A WISDOM-DRIVEN LIFE

+ The wisdom journey introduces us to ourselves.

+ The wisdom journey aids in our personal development.

+ The wisdom journey brings people into our life who can help us, especially at important junctures.

+ The wisdom journey prepares us for our destination, or the fulfillment of our purpose.

APPLYING WISDOM

1. In what ways has the journey of life introduced you to yourself?

2. Name a difficult situation that helped to prepare you for later events or made you a stronger person. If you're going through a challenging situation right now, what wisdom or knowledge can you glean from it?

3. Identify several people who have already been key in helping you move forward in life or to attain achievements. Why not thank them for their positive influence in your life?

4. How can you better prepare for future opportunities that will move you toward the fulfillment of your purpose?

PART 2
WISDOM STRENGTHENS OUR POSITION

4

WISDOM PLANS AHEAD

You don't get what you want in life—
you get what you prepare for.

The cause of most failures in life is a lack of preparation. We think we're ready to begin a project or an endeavor, or we think we can keep a current venture going, only to have everything fall apart—for the simple and avoidable reason that we haven't adequately prepared for it. We haven't thought through all the implications or problems that might arise and how to address them. If we don't have a plan, the best we can hope for is a hit-or-miss chance of success. Two popular adages highlight this truth: "If you don't know where you are going in life, any road will take you there," and "When you fail to plan, you plan to fail."

Wisdom tells us that the time to *be* ready is not the time to *get* ready. At that point, it might be too late. The groundwork has to be done ahead of time.

BENEFITS OF PLANNING

Preparation is the greatest evidence that we believe something better is coming into our life. And the bigger that something is going to be, the more time we need to prepare for it. When we understand the benefits of planning and how to go about it, we can accomplish much while avoiding unnecessary disappointment and undue stress. So let's begin by looking at some specific benefits we derive from planning.

WISDOM TELLS US THAT THE TIME TO *BE* READY IS
NOT THE TIME TO *GET* READY.

WE LIVE LIFE ACCORDING TO OUR PURPOSE, NOT OTHERS' IDEAS OR INTENTIONS

The first benefit of planning is that it enables us to follow through with what we have identified as our life's purpose. If we don't have a plan for what we want to do, we might live somebody else's plan for our lives rather than our true calling, because we are following the path of least resistance. The person who has no strategy will always be at the mercy of the one who has a strategy and is ready to draw others into it, whether it is aligned with their purpose or not.

WE GIVE A GOOD FOUNDATION FOR ALL OUR ENDEAVORS

Second, for the implementation of any idea or initiative, planning gives us a solid foundation to build on. For example, no one who wants to start a business will be successful in the long run without a well-thought-out business plan. Suppose you wanted to apply for a bank loan to open up a café? You would need to develop a detailed proposal so the bank could determine if you have thought through all the relevant elements and details of the venture—even down to the specific types of sandwiches that would be served and a list of their ingredients—to decide whether you have a good chance for success.

What specifics have you identified as being necessary for your own dreams to become reality? First, do you have a clear strategy for fulfilling your life's purpose? Within that framework, if you want to get married, what's your plan? If you want to obtain more education, what's your plan? If you want to take a sabbatical and travel, what's your plan? Have you thought through all the details of what you desire to accomplish?

"WHEN YOU FAIL TO PLAN, YOU PLAN TO FAIL."

WE ANTICIPATE AND DEVELOP RESPONSES TO POTENTIAL PROBLEMS

I like the "plan ahead" acrostic that John Maxwell uses, which includes the anticipation of future needs:

PLAN:

+ Predetermine a course of action.

+ Lay out your goals.

+ Adjust your priorities.

+ Notify key personnel.

AHEAD:

+ Allow time for acceptance.

+ Head into action.

+ Expect problems.

+ Always point to the successes.

+ Daily review your plan.[11]

---

11. See John Maxwell, *The 21 Irrefutable Laws of Leadership*, rev. ed. (Nashville: Thomas Nelson 2007), 43.

Although all these points are valuable, I want to focus here on "Expect problems." This is where many people miss it while pursuing their dreams and goals. They go into an endeavor wide-eyed and optimistic, overlooking the fact that we live in a problematic world where issues arise that must be addressed. Planning gives us the foresight to identify potential needs and problems before we experience them, so that we can prepare for as many eventualities as possible and know in advance the course of action we will take if difficulties arise.

Optimism is a wonderful quality, and we will talk more about its importance later on in this book. But optimism and practicality have to go together. Although I consider myself to be "Mr. Positivity," I don't believe it is negative thinking to anticipate that things are not always going to proceed according to the way we want them to or have planned for them to go. Certain things will come up in life that are totally unexpected.

I have noticed that some people are under the impression that their faith or optimism will enable them to *avoid* problems rather than empower them to go *through* them. Yet Jesus Himself said, "In this world you will have trouble. But take heart! I have overcome the world."[12] It is not a sign of faithlessness to anticipate problems, because we are guaranteed to have various troubles in life. We just need to decide how we will respond to them.

Here's a simple illustration of how having optimism alone can cause people to fail. Suppose someone wanted to open a particular kind of store. Having little experience in business, they imagine that if they get a hundred customers each day, and every customer spends at least ten dollars, they'll receive a thousand dollars of gross income daily. Even if they do get a hundred people in their store every day, not everyone will purchase something. Many will come in and just browse. The business owner will have to revise their estimate of daily income after doing detailed market research, and even then there is no guarantee the projected sales will be met. Sales might be higher or lower than anticipated. Thus, for such endeavors, part of the planning process would be to factor in that some people won't be interested in what you have to offer and that you must expect to deal with a certain amount of rejection.

12. John 16:33 (NIV).

Moreover, the business owner would have to realize that a lack of response to a particular product doesn't necessarily mean the product is bad, but only that it needs to be targeted to the best audience and presented to enough people. There are about seven billion people on the planet. This means that if you produce something and get rejected by even a million people, there may still be a big market for it. Suppose the very thing that you're gifted in producing will be huge in Asia or Europe, and you haven't even gotten your product advertised there yet. You may simply be fishing in the wrong waters. Having a well-thought-out plan helps us to avoid wasting time and money on efforts that are bound to be unprofitable. If this does happen, we need to immediately revise our game plan, analyzing, "What's wrong with what I'm doing? What am I overlooking? What new markets can I explore?"

Thus, when we plan anything—from something as small as a local family gathering to something as huge as a merger of major corporations—we should always anticipate that we may be confronted by unexpected or negative developments. Ask yourself, "What if this (idea, plan, operation, project, relationship) doesn't work? Should I put all of my eggs in this one basket?" Make a plan for what you will do if something falls through. For example, in regard to your business or vocation, you might ask yourself questions such as these: "What if I'm not hired for this particular job?" "What if the company doesn't renew their contract with me?" "What if the cost of my goods goes up?" "What if one of my vice presidents quits?" "What if my product is no longer popular or needed?"

Again, asking such questions doesn't mean you're being pessimistic or distrustful—just practical. Remember that if human beings are involved in anything, there will be problems! Some things are not a matter of if but when.

If you consider these types of issues up front, it will help you to strategize wisely. Your plan needs to address as many scenarios as possible, as well as what types of resources are available in case the unexpected happens. If your perspective has been based purely on optimism, you have to wake up and smell the coffee, because you lack a sound plan for success.

WE SAVE RESOURCES FOR LEAN TIMES

Additionally, planning ahead encourages us to store up during seasons of plenty so that we can continue to have a source of supply during times of lack. Many individuals, businesses, and organizations spend everything they have in the present without considering possible shortages in the future. Instead of encouraging us to save for scarce times, today's society so relentlessly advocates spending that it's very easy to get caught up in overspending.

One definition of poverty is using everything you have in one generation (this applies not only to material resources, but also to spiritual, intellectual, emotional, and physical ones) so that, when the next generation comes, there is no inheritance for them to build on. This is how many families get stuck in a low economic class or a negative emotional outlook. We should make plans to reserve finances and preserve other resources that will be necessary for us—and our families—to maintain, grow, and thrive throughout the course of our lives.

TODAY WELL LIVED WILL TAKE CARE OF TOMORROW.

WE KEEP GOING EVEN WHEN OUR ENTHUSIASM FAILS

Planning also helps us to keep going during those times when, temporarily, our motivation grows weak and our enthusiasm fades. One NFL team owner promised all his players a brand new Cadillac if they won the Super Bowl. The players were filled with enthusiasm over that prospect, but they went out and lost the game anyway. Is enthusiasm important? Absolutely. But enthusiasm alone will not win the victory. To have the best chance at winning, a sports team needs to diligently prepare its game plan ahead of time by formulating an effective strategy based on a close study of itself and its opponents and making sure that strategy is clear to all team members, by conducting training exercises that develop team members' strength and endurance, and by honing the specific skills of individual athletes. The team has to practice various plays continually and under different conditions until those plays become second nature and can be performed even under intense pressure.

TWO THINGS CAN DRAMATICALLY REDUCE
YOUR FEAR OF DOING ANYTHING:
PREPARATION AND PRACTICE.

We develop skills by learning to do them correctly and then repeating them over and over. The more we practice them, the easier it will be for us to do them right when it really counts. Skills become automatic as we form habits. This principle applies to any important scenario that we need to anticipate and prepare for. For example, many school systems and places of business are required to have regular fire drills; their safety procedures include planning out and practicing what students and teachers or employees will do in case of a fire or other emergency. Through repeated simulated circumstances, people's responses become like a reflex. When you are in the middle of a crisis, you don't have time to start thinking about what the best course of action should be. You have to be trained for it ahead of time. It's has to be in your muscle memory that "when this happens, this is what I do." The only way to get to that place is to plan and practice.

Similarly, by making specific plans to reach the goals we have set, regularly reviewing those goals, and continually training ourselves in what is required to implement them, we can keep focused on the ongoing skills and preparation we need for success. Practice doesn't always make perfect, but it does make better. Give yourself a chance to learn and to grow. Then, as you are working toward your goals, if your enthusiasm temporarily weakens or falls short, or any other problems arise, you will have strong preparation to fall back on and a trained mind-set that will enable you to persevere and keep moving forward so you can be successful in the end.

WE REGAIN OUR STRIDE IF WE STUMBLE AND FALL

Anyone can make a mistake, and we may fall flat on our face doing the very best we can. But we have to remember that falling does not disqualify a runner from a race; they can always get up again and keep running. If we fall, we cannot just lie there and make excuses or blame other people for what happened, or we will stay in that fallen position and have no chance at finishing well. Instead, we need to remind ourselves, "I have to get up because I have a race I *must* finish."

Additionally, it's one thing to get back up again when you fall; it's another thing to regain your stride and keep pressing forward. So if you make a misstep, evaluate what went wrong and make corrections and adjustments to your plan, but then look again to the unfolding of your purpose and goals. If you have fallen behind your original timetable, you may be able to lengthen your strides while keeping your eyes on the goal. Maintain your determination to run so that you can succeed.

KEYS FOR STRATEGIC PLANNING

We can summarize the above points with this simple but indispensable truth: planning gives us the opportunity to prepare for success and to prevent failure. When we have a clear strategy for fulfilling our purpose, we can move forward to a make positive difference in our life and the lives of others. Sometimes, we don't need to be informed about wisdom principles as much we need to regularly remind ourselves of the principles we already know, because it is only when we actually put the principles into action that they can help us. Too often, we leap into endeavors without planning for them, even though we supposedly know the benefits of having a strategy and goals. It won't do just to "know" we need to plan—we must start planning.

Here are some foundational keys for strategic planning to help ensure that your plans are well thought out and have a strong basis for success. Some endeavors are simple and require only simple plans; others are more complex and require comprehensive plans. Apply the following keys in a way that is appropriate to your particular endeavor and scale of operation.

1. DEFINE YOUR VISION AND MISSION

As you consider how to pursue your purpose, or as you start to plan any significant endeavor, it's important to define your vision and mission in relation to it. You may know your purpose in general terms, but a vision statement expresses the way you intend to fulfill that purpose according to your particular focus, gift, and interests. A mission statement gets even more specific about how you intend to carry out your vision. Both of these statements should be as unambiguous as possible, avoiding vague or competing objectives.

To clarify, here is an example of the difference between purpose, vision, and mission. Suppose two people have a similar life purpose of promoting literacy. The first person has a vision for running a nonprofit organization that teaches adults to read, while the second person has a vision of teaching reading skills to children. The first person has a mission statement that clearly outlines how they will serve the needs of nonreading adults through a storefront community center in a particular neighborhood in the inner city where they live. The second person has a mission statement that details how they will develop an afterschool program staffed by volunteer instructors consisting of current or retired English teachers who will conduct reading tutorials at libraries in specific towns in a particular region. Each person has a passion for literacy, but each has a special way of expressing and serving that general purpose.

Difference Between Purpose, Vision, and Mission	
Person A	Person B
PURPOSE: Promoting Literacy	
VISION: Running a nonprofit organization that teaches adults to read.	VISION: Teaching reading skills to children.
Mission: To serve the needs of nonreading adults through a storefront community center in a particular neighborhood in the inner city.	Mission: To develop an afterschool program staffed by volunteer instructors consisting of current or retired English teachers who will conduct reading tutorials at libraries in specific towns in a particular region.

When you develop your vision and mission statements, be sure to envision what might be, not just what present circumstances indicate is doable. Imagine the possibilities. You have to define the "what" and the "why" before you can figure out the "how."

2. ASSESS YOUR SITUATION AND COUNT THE COST

As you settle on a specific focus and develop your mission statement, a key part of your strategic planning will be to review your current situation, assessing your gifts, strengths, accomplishments, skills, weaknesses, and needs in relation to what you want to do. You need to understand realistically what you are dealing with, asking yourself, "What will I have to overcome to fulfill my plan?" In this process, you must count the cost in several ways. First, how much will it literally cost in terms of money and other resources? Second, how much will it cost in terms of mental, emotional, and physical energy? And are you willing to pay that price? Third, what will it cost in terms of your priorities? We often fail because we put more attention and energy on secondary things than on primary ones. Will you be able to put first things first?

NOTHING WILL MOVE FORWARD
UNTIL YOU SCHEDULE IT.

3. DECIDE ON A PLAN OF ACTION WITH CONCRETE GOALS

The next thing is to put together a specific plan of action based on your vision and mission statements and on what you have determined you need to succeed. Figure out exactly what is required. Organize yourself. Include a detailed listing of the resources and equipment that will be necessary, even if they will be acquired gradually. You have to become familiar with the necessary tools and be comfortable and skilled at using them—or find others who can do that. When seasoned chefs prepare to cook, they first line up all their ingredients rather than searching for ingredients as they go. Likewise, you should take inventory ahead of time and be sure to have all your resources ready when you need them.

You also need to set concrete goals. A goal can be defined as a dream with a deadline. You must first establish a plan, but nothing will move forward until you schedule it. Outline what you will do step-by-step. You can always revise the deadlines as needed, but if you don't have goals, you won't make much progress.

4. DETERMINE AND BUILD THE NECESSARY TEAM

Part of developing your plan of action is to ask yourself, "What other people are needed in order for this endeavor to come off properly, and what perspectives and skills should they have?" Strategizing in this way will help ensure that you have the appropriate partners and teammates in place, whether they are directly associated with you or function in supporting capacities. For example, when you get ready to initiate your plan, you don't need people on your team who are afraid you're going to fail. You need realistic people, not mere naysayers; you need people who can exercise discernment while also seeing the possibilities. Neither do you need those who will intimidate other team members to fulfill their own agendas; you want people who have conviction but are also able to express their views in harmony with the overall purpose, vision, and team. Additionally, it's not only a matter of getting the right people on board generally—you have to get the right people in the right seats. That requires a careful evaluation of people's individual strengths.

In the process of applying these first four keys to strategic planning, discuss your ideas with others. Don't implement something that you haven't fully thought out and tested in some way, or that you haven't presented to other people who either have experience in that area or have done something similar. (The exception to this might be with something truly groundbreaking that no one has attempted before; then you have to trust your instincts while relying on the best plans you can develop.) Remember, those who have already been where you want to go can save you a lot of time and money by relating to you their experience and wisdom.

5. ADD TO YOUR KNOWLEDGE AND EXPERIENCE

As you make your plans (and even as you begin to implement them), you also need to determine if you need additional education or training to be able to complete them. If so, schedule when you will get the education or training and make the appropriate arrangements; it may be necessary for you to plan how you will obtain the additional funds needed to go back to school or to receive the training. Additionally, seek to gain further hands-on experience that will move you closer to being able to fulfill your goals.

6. EXECUTE YOUR PLAN

We have seen that having a plan is not sufficient if we never execute that plan. As the saying goes, "Plan your work, and then work your plan." But we begin to work our plan when we have correctly positioned ourselves to do so.

When runners are at the starting line of a race, they don't just suddenly begin running whenever they feel like it. They have to wait for the announcer's directions. We can compare those directions to the way planning and implementation works. Step number one is "On your mark...." The announcer doesn't say, "On somebody else's mark...." It's on *your* mark. That's why you may start pursuing a goal at a later age than someone else did. Don't get confused about that. It doesn't matter if they did it in their twenties and you are now in your sixties. Forget that. It's on *your* mark.

The second step is "Get set...," which means "Be prepared to move." You have to be in a certain position where you are ready to run; you can't just take off standing straight. Many times, you can tell whether somebody is ready for something by their posture. There are people who think they are ready to go when they're actually not in position for it.

Then, it's "Go!" Sometimes we have to remind ourselves, "I'm not going to live forever. If I don't start working on this right now, it may never get done." There are some things we can begin to do even while waiting for other things to be ready. Whenever you are positioned to do something, take action.

After you get started, review your plans regularly to make sure you stay on track and to determine any needed modifications. Failure follows a lack of planning and follow-through. But good results follow a carefully executed plan.

WE NEED TO BE IN THE RIGHT POSTURE, READY TO MOVE, IN ORDER TO EXECUTE OUR PLAN.

BENEFITS OF A WISDOM-DRIVEN LIFE

+ When we plan ahead:
  › We live according to our purpose, not according to the arbitrary ideas or intentions of others.
  › We give a good foundation for our endeavors.
  › We develop responses to potential problems and save resources for lean times.
  › We keep going even when our enthusiasm fails, and we rejoin the race if we stumble and fall.
+ Strategic planning keeps us on track; it enables us to define our vision and mission, assess our situation and count the cost, decide on a plan of action and concrete goals, build the necessary team, add to our knowledge and experience, and execute our plan.

APPLYING WISDOM

1. Write out vision and mission statements that correspond to your purpose.
2. Assess where you are in life—including your gifts, strengths, accomplishments, skills, weaknesses, and needs—in relation to what you want to do.

3. Work on a plan of action and goals that aligns with your mission statement, acknowledging the resources needed and the various costs of getting where you need to go.

4. Determine which other people/roles you will need in order to carry out your plan, whether they are directly associated with you or in supporting capacities.

5. Identify any additional education or training you may need to fulfill your vision and schedule when you will obtain it.

6. When you are in position, take specific action steps to begin to implement your plan, and review your progress regularly.

5

WISDOM CREATES WINNING HABITS, PART 1: THE POWER OF HABIT

Habits shape our character,
and our character determines our destiny.

Success has a great deal to do with habit. Essentially, winning is the combination of positive habits, while losing is the combination of negative habits—as well as the neglect of good habits. The challenge we face is that good habits must be formed, while bad habits are easily fallen into. The maxim known as "Eng's Principle" says, "The easier it is to do, the harder it is to change." Something that's easy to get into is often difficult to get out of.

We are all creatures of habit, whether those habits are predominately positive or negative—or a mixture. And hidden in the routine of our habits is the prophecy of where we're going. We can only become tomorrow what we are becoming today.

Every one of us can admit to having some negative habits that need to be broken. (If you are ever in doubt about that, just ask the people you are in relationship with!) There is a Spanish proverb that says, "Habits are first cobwebs and then cables." They start out lightweight, easy to get rid of; but after a while they become like thick cables, hard to break. As Samuel Johnson pointed out, "The chains of habit are generally too small to be felt until they are too strong to be broken." That statement is true—to a point. But I don't think the bonds created by bad habits are always too strong to be severed; they can still be broken by faith and diligence. I believe in the power of God to help us to dismantle bad habits in our lives. Although we may need professional assistance at times, we are not a victim of our habits to the degree that we cannot break them and build new and better habits.

The good news is that we can set our lives on a winning course by intentionally discarding practices that hinder us and by developing practices that enable us to move forward and prosper. Keep in mind that no matter how much we learn about wise living and good habits, our life will not change until we apply what we've learned. Change can be uncomfortable at times, but it is necessary for developing positive practices. Charles Kettering said, "The world hates change, and yet it's the only thing that has brought progress." So if we don't like the way a certain aspect of our life is going, or if we don't like the general direction of our life, we need to change our habits. We can create positive habits that will help us to become better at, and better for, our purpose in life. Remember this: we have the power to choose what our habits will be.

SUCCESS IS FOUND IN DAILY ROUTINES

All habits are established through repetition. You don't become successful at something by doing it just one time. You succeed by doing it on a regular basis. Each time we repeat an act, we strengthen the habit. That is why we need to build a pattern by which we absorb positive practices into our life. Thus, while success may not come in a day, success is found in daily routines. As Robert Collier said, "Success is the sum of small efforts repeated day in and day out." And Aristotle said, "We are what we repeatedly do. Excellence then is not an act but a habit."

When you see a person who is self-disciplined, you know they have taken the time to develop good habits. They have a mind-set that embraces the benefits of submitting to discipline. Sybil Stanton, author of *The 25-Hour Woman*, said, "True discipline isn't on your back needling you with imperatives; it's at your side, nudging you with incentives. When you understand that discipline is self-caring, not self-castigating, you won't cringe at its mention, but will cultivate it."[13]

WE HAVE THE POWER TO CHOOSE WHAT OUR HABITS WILL BE.

That's really what discipline is. It is not self-castigating, or punishing yourself. It is self-caring. We don't have to wince at it because it's not there merely to stand over us with commands, but it's at our side encouraging us with all the powerful benefits that result from being a person of discipline. If you're going to become good at something, it's because you welcome discipline as a means of getting you there. Regardless of what role you're preparing to fulfill or what outcome you're working toward, the discipline of developing positive practices will move you closer to your goal.

Musical virtuosos are not made by sitting back and admiring somebody else's gift. They have to practice their craft day in and day out, hour upon hour. You can easily tell the difference between a professional who has applied time and discipline to their talent, and an amateur who merely dabbles in their talent. You may have heard the story about the individual who heard a virtuoso play and then said, "I'd give my life to be able to play like that!" The musician replied, "I did give my life, eight hours a day for forty years, practicing!" Sometimes you can tell how hungry you are for something by what you're willing to give up in order to get it.

---

13. Sybil Stanton, *The 25-Hour Woman* (New York: Bantam, 1990).

HOW HABITS DEVELOP

Most people develop habits—both positive and negative—through a rather unconscious process. That process follows what Shad Helmstetter outlines in his classic book *What to Say When You Talk to Your Self*:

> In logical progression, what we believe determines our attitudes, affects our feelings, directs our behavior, and determines our success or failure.
>
> *1. Programming creates beliefs.*
>
> *2. Beliefs create attitudes.*
>
> *3. Attitudes create feelings.*
>
> *4. Feelings determine actions.*
>
> *5. Actions create results.*[14]

I will sum up Helmstetter's points as we explore these statements in relation to habit.

OUR "PROGRAMMING" SETS UP OUR BELIEFS

It all begins with how we think about ourselves and about life—with how our mind has been "programmed" to think.

> What we have accepted from the outside world, or fed to ourselves, has initiated a natural cause-and-effect reaction sequence that leads us either to successful self-management, or to the unsuccessful mismanagement of ourselves, our resources, and our future.
>
> It is our programming that sets up our beliefs, and the chain reaction begins.[15]

While we all react in different ways to the people and circumstances in our lives, these influences can have a major effect on the philosophies and ideologies we accept, and therefore the habits we form in life. Our beliefs may be programmed by any or all of the following:

---

14. Shad Helmstetter, Ph.D., *What to Say When You Talk to Your Self*, rev. ed. (New York: Gallery Books [Simon & Shuster, Inc.], 2017), 52–53. Italics are in the original.
15. Ibid, 52.

+ The people around us who are models and examples for us, particularly while we are growing up. For instance, if a child is raised in a household where the mother or father has a bad temper, they are often programmed to react with anger whenever they are frustrated, scared, or confused.

+ The words that are spoken to us—particularly repetitiously. We might form habits based on ideas about ourselves that are continuously reinforced by the words of a person of influence in our life, whether those words are "You have great potential!" or "You're a nobody!"

+ The ways in which people treat us. We might develop positive or negative habits based on whether we are treated with respect, disdain, or apathy.

+ The expectations of our culture to act or look a specific way or to value certain things. For example, we might accept an underlying cultural idea that style is more important than substance for getting ahead in life, and therefore develop habits that reinforce that outlook.

+ The messages of the media we absorb, such as TV, radio, social media, books, or magazines. If we see that "everyone" on social media is doing a particular activity or thinking a certain way, we might make a habit of doing the same thing.

+ How we absorb, assimilate, and apply the sum total of our learning and experiences in life.

We might have been programmed in such a way that we mismanage just one area of our lives, several areas, or most areas. That is why a person might be successful in their vocation but not in their relationships, or vice versa.

In what ways have these various elements influenced your own life habits? As Shad Helmstetter points out, we respond to life based on what we think. Belief does not require something to be true; it only requires us to think that it's true. In this way, what a person thinks about events can be far more important than the events themselves.[16] That's how a lie can become an assumed truth to a person. Stephen Covey said, "The way we see the problem is the problem." Thus, you have to be careful what beliefs you formulate and accept, recognizing how they affect your actions, including your daily habits—because what you think about is what you will bring about.

WHAT YOU THINK ABOUT IS WHAT YOU WILL BRING ABOUT.

OUR BELIEFS CREATE OUR ATTITUDES

The way we've been programmed determines our belief system, and our beliefs subsequently control our attitudes. Our attitudes are what make up our frame of mind.

Faulty attitudes are like a flat tire. You aren't going anywhere until you fix them. Some people can't change their lives simply because they won't fix their attitudes. William James, one of the most pragmatic psychologists I have ever read, wrote, "Human beings, by changing the inner attitudes of their minds, can change the outer aspects of their lives." Solomon said much the same thing when he wrote, "As [a person] thinks in his heart, so is he."[17]

In a sense, there are things that your heart knows that your head knows nothing about. We usually gravitate to whatever desires are secretly in our heart. If you have a particular job but your heart is secretly longing to be at a different job, you will probably end up at that different job. It's more important where your heart is than where your body is.

I believe the difference between head thinking and heart thinking has to do with depth. The deepest thinking happens in your heart, and that's

---

16. Ibid., 50.
17. Proverbs 23:7.

why we need to start paying attention to the thoughts of our heart, particularly as they influence our habits.

OUR ATTITUDES CREATE OUR FEELINGS

Our attitudes affect our feelings toward ourselves, our parents, our spouse, our coworkers, our abilities, our potential, and everything else in life. If we have the attitude that the world is against us, it can lead to feelings of anger, resentment, and discouragement. If we have the attitude that we have been wronged but we're not going to let that prevent us from being happy and fulfilling our purpose, then we can nurture positive feelings of love and hope while building a good and productive life.

OUR FEELINGS DETERMINE OUR ACTIONS

When we fall into negative outlooks and emotions, it can lead us to negative behaviors if we haven't learned to resist the temptation to act merely according to how we feel. For example, perhaps we were neglected by our parents at an early age and our emotional needs were not met. As a result, our lingering wounded feelings cause us to try to meet those needs in self-destructive ways. This is how many people develop addictions.

Feelings often make it hard for us to break bad habits and be consistent in developing good habits. With most people, if they don't feel like doing something, it won't get done. And no matter how good our intentions, there are some days when we just don't feel like doing something we should do. We have to develop the practice of doing what is best for us no matter how we feel. It takes determination and maturity to follow through when we aren't motivated to do something.

Since feelings come from attitudes, when we change our attitudes, we can alter our feelings and consequently our behavior. For instance, if I love someone and am in a relationship with them, my commitment of love toward that person (not just my "feelings" of love) will cause me to do what's best for them, even if I am not "in the mood" to do it. That's why a mother will get up in the middle of the night and take care of a sick child when she is exhausted and perhaps sick herself. She is self-sacrificing because she has adopted the attitude that this is what a mother does when she loves her child, and that attitude motivates her to act.

Ask yourself, "How do my feelings influence my actions—or my lack of action?" Think about various life situations, and for each situation answer these questions: "When _____ happens, how do I usually behave? What is motivating my behavior? What have been the outcomes of my behavior?"

OUR ACTIONS OR INACTIONS CREATE RESULTS

Finally, the results in our lives are largely the accumulation of both the actions we take and the actions we do not take. If we don't sow good seeds, we can't expect a good harvest. Plus, we can talk about something all we want, but actions bring about results.

> "WE FIRST MAKE OUR HABITS,
> AND THEN OUR HABITS MAKE US."
> — JOHN DRYDEN

GOOD HABITS SERVE US, WHILE BAD HABITS DOMINATE US

Keep in mind that the process we just looked at can yield either positive or negative results, depending on the beliefs we have accepted and live out. This is the process by which winning or losing has become established in the various areas of our lives. If someone has followed a predominately negative path in line with this pattern, they may have tried to break bad habits in the past, but they have probably failed in the attempt. It's as if they keep getting out the broom and tearing down the cobwebs in their life, but they never deal with the spider, or the false beliefs that have led to their negative feelings and actions. If we tear down the web but leave the spider intact, the spider will just spin another web.

Nathaniel Emmons said, "Habit is either the best of servants or the worst of masters." When you have a good habit, it is a wonderful servant, but when you have a bad habit, it's a terrible master. Wrong habits are debilitating because they keep us stagnant at best or headed toward destruction at worst. We cannot grow or make progress if we are dominated by wrong habits.

As I mentioned at the beginning of the chapter, the process by which we develop habits is usually unconscious for us. But we can change that by paying more attention to how our habits have been formed, and by becoming more intentional about developing positive habits. Some psychologists believe that up to 95 percent of our behavior is formed through habit. We need to learn to *choose* our habits, because our habits lead to our future. We will either live our life by design or by default. Living by default not only won't get us where we want to go, but it is also unfulfilling and frustrating.

In general, it's not that successful people are so much more talented than others or have a considerably different nature. It's just that most of them have better habits. Their habits make them. Confucius said, "Men's natures are alike, but it is their habits that separate them." Like most people, successful people don't always feel like getting up early, but they have developed the habit of getting up early in order to pursue their purpose with passion, enabling them to continually make progress toward fulfilling it. They don't always feel like working hard and denying themselves certain things and making sacrifices today to achieve a greater goal in the future. The difference is that they have the habit of doing not what they "want" to do but what they need to do.

In the end, creating winning habits is ultimately about shaping our character. Habits shape our character, and our character determines our destiny. Fyodor Dostoyevsky pointed out, "The second half of a man's life is made up of nothing but the habits that he has acquired during the first half." If we have developed some bad habits to this point in our life, their effects will be felt by us sooner or later—unless we learn to change those habits and develop new, positive ones. If we have developed some good practices but want to build on them with additional practices that will enable us to become stronger and go higher, we need to know more specifics about how to purposely develop positive habits. Both needs will be addressed in the next chapter.

WHEN YOU HAVE A GOOD HABIT,
IT IS A WONDERFUL SERVANT, BUT WHEN YOU
HAVE A BAD HABIT, IT IS A TERRIBLE MASTER.

BENEFITS OF A WISDOM-DRIVEN LIFE

+ Developing positive habits will enable us to win in life.

+ Success is found in daily routines.

+ Positive practices help us become better at, and better for, our purpose.

+ Positive habits lead us to become successful self-managers of our lives.

+ A good habit is a wonderful servant.

+ Habits shape our character, and character determines our destiny.

APPLYING WISDOM

1. Think about a positive habit you have formed in your life. Can you trace the "programming," beliefs, attitudes, and feelings that led you to develop it?

2. Now think about a negative habit you have formed. Can you trace how it developed?

3. What do you think of the statement, "The results in our lives are largely the accumulation of both the actions we take and the actions we do not take"? In your personal experience, has that statement proven to be true? If so, in what ways?

6

WISDOM CREATES WINNING HABITS, PART 2: POSITIVE PRACTICES FOR SUCCESS

You can only become tomorrow
what you are becoming today.

As we pursue the wisdom-driven life, we can make a conscious effort to cultivate good habits while weeding out bad habits that undermine and even plague us. We can establish stronger patterns of doing what is positive, edifying, and productive.

When is the best time to break a bad habit? Right now! There is a Yiddish proverb that says, "Bad habits are easier to abandon today than tomorrow." Why? Because if we wait, they will have another day to dig their tentacles a little deeper into our lives. If you say, "I am going to stop doing _____ some day," that's not sufficient because it will probably never happen. Thomas Merton said, "We must make the choices that enable us to fulfill the deepest capacities of our real selves."

BREAKING BAD HABITS AND DEVELOPING GOOD HABITS

Many people want immediate change, but such transformation is more the exception than the rule. Remember that change is a process, not an event. Dropping a bad habit or developing a positive habit is seldom instantaneous. It comes little by little. Change actually works better when it is a process, because during the course of dropping an old habit or establishing a new one, you build the necessary "muscles" that enable you to walk in a sustained pattern of positive living. This allows you to continue to move forward without slipping back into the old behavior.

There are specific ways in which we can work toward permanent change in our habits. The following are the means by which you can establish positive practices for success, enabling you to fulfill your purpose and goals in life.

TAKE INVENTORY

First, take inventory of your life by asking yourself seven simple questions:

1. What have I done right in the past?

2. Where have I gone wrong?

3. What have I learned from my past experiences?

4. Where do I want to go?

5. What will get me there?

6. Does my current daily routine prophesy that I will arrive at my desired destination—or that I will fall short of getting there?

7. What can I do better or differently starting now?

When you assess your failures, please be encouraged, because our failures often teach us much more than our successes. Whatever mistakes you have made, they were not in vain if you can learn something from them. It's not about, "What did I go through?" but rather "What did I *grow* through?"

On the Internet, there are various versions of a list entitled "Rules for Being Human."[18] Here are five rules from those lists that apply to assessing where we are in life:

+ You will learn lessons.

+ There are no mistakes, only lessons.

+ If you don't learn the easy lessons, they get harder.

+ A lesson that is not learned must be repeated.

+ You will know you have learned the lesson when your actions change.

So let us glean not only from our past successes but also from our defeats, and then move on from them. Remember, when you change your habits, you can actually change your destiny.

MAKE AN INTENTIONAL DECISION TO CHANGE

After taking inventory of your life, realize that all change begins with a decision. A decision to change is an act of your will, not a reaction of your emotions. The reason we need to be intentional about changing our negative habits is that habit is stronger than reason. A person can know they shouldn't do something, but habit prompts them to do it anyway. We have to make a definite choice to break a bad habit or develop a good habit. Doing so may be a simultaneous process because breaking a negative habit often involves substituting it with a positive habit.

Thus, we make a decision that we will break the habit of spending more money than we take in, or envying other people, or lying or gossiping, or abusing drugs or alcohol, or another negative practice. We make a conscious decision to discard the old way and to begin to act in a different way with a new behavior. Likewise, to develop a good habit, such as taking a certain amount of time each day or each week to build a new business, write a book, exercise, or organize our office, we make an intentional decision to incorporate that new habit into our life. To be really successful at

---

18. "Ten Rules for Being Human" are attributed to Chérie Carter-Scott, a corporate trainer and consultant. They were published in the original *Chicken Soup for the Soul* and then expanded on in Carter-Scott's *If Life Is a Game, These Are the Rules* (New York: Penguin Random House: 1998). Three of the "rules" included in this chapter are found on her list.

developing a habit and sticking to our decision, we should choose a simple habit and build from there.

Making specific decisions about our mind-set and behavior is the way to build positive practices in our life. The word *decision* comes from the Latin word *decidere*, which literally means "to cut off." So remember that any time you make a decision, it means that you cut off other options or ways in order to follow the new option or way.

"IF WE LEAVE OUR LIVES UP TO CHANCE, CHANCES ARE, WE'LL FAIL." —SHAD HELMSTETTER[19]

DO IT FOR YOURSELF, NOT TO IMPRESS OR APPEASE OTHERS

Be careful not to quit a bad habit or develop a good habit in order to impress or appease somebody else. You don't change for other people, even though your changing may benefit them. Why? If you're not doing it for yourself, the change will probably not last, and you may become resentful toward the person for whom you tried to change. Even if the change does hold, the other person might not appreciate your efforts, and you might grow disheartened and give up because of their lack of affirmation. Additionally, if you develop a habit for someone else's sake, you may always feel like the other person owes you something. So do it for yourself. You're the one who will reap the highest benefit from it, becoming transformed in the process.

DEVELOP A PLAN

Once you make the decision to change something in your life for your own sake, you need a clear plan to carry it out. This is where you can incorporate some planning principles from the chapter "Wisdom Plans Ahead."

19. *What to Say*, 45.

Change won't happen just because you say, "Next year is going to be my year!" It's not only what you say that makes it so. That's the beginning of it, because you need to declare your intentions, but you also must have a specific plan. For example, if you want to become more fiscally responsible, you need a plan for establishing a budget and reducing debt. There are many resources in print or electronic form to help you in the specifics of developing a financial plan. Or, if you want to lose weight, you need to put together a diet and exercise program, consulting your doctor or another health professional as you start and continue the process.

SET ACHIEVABLE GOALS

Next, set achievable goals based on your plan that can be measured. We can easily become discouraged if we try to bite off something too big for us to accomplish or if we aren't tracking our progress. Again, start with small goals and work up to larger ones. So, for example, if you've never had a habit of running for exercise but want to develop that ability, you shouldn't expect to immediately take off and run like Olympic sprinter Usain Bolt. We need to take small but significant steps toward success. The Chinese have a saying, "Be not afraid of growing slowly; only be afraid of standing still."

As you set goals, use the "SMART" plan. This means developing goals that are *specific, measurable, attainable, realistic,* and *time-sensitive.*

1. Goals must be specific. If it's not specific, it's not a goal. You don't say, "I'm going to lose *some* weight." How much weight? Ten, twenty, thirty pounds? If you don't make your goal definite, you won't know whether or not you have achieved it.

2. Goals must be measurable. Decide what measure you will use to track your progress, and how often will you assess that progress.

3. Goals must be attainable—by you. You shouldn't set a goal you can't personally attain (though don't sell yourself short). We don't need to try to attain something that is somebody else's purpose and vision. We will end up failing and wonder what happened. So seek what is attainable for you—for who you are and what you are designed for. It goes back to purpose—the purpose in your heart will help guide you in determining your long-term capabilities.

4. Goals must be realistic. This may seem like a repeat of number three, but let me give you an example of the difference between something being attainable and something being realistic. In the mid-twentieth century, when humankind decided to go to the moon, that was an attainable goal because we were developing the capability to do it through the available knowledge and technology. Before that time, the idea had seemed like science fiction. In the early 1960s, the Soviet Union sent the first man into space, and America followed by not only putting men in space but also sending men to the moon by 1969. The goal was attainable, but it wouldn't have been realistic to try to put a man on the moon after merely two weeks of research into space travel. And it wouldn't have been realistic for America to attempt to send astronauts to the moon before doing preliminary flights in which astronauts orbited the earth.

IN ORDER TO CHANGE YOUR LIFE, YOU HAVE TO CHANGE YOUR WAYS.

When determining whether a goal is realistic, then, we do the best we can with the knowledge and experience we have. We may well end up going beyond what initially seems realistic to us and others, but we need to begin somewhere.

5. Goals must be time-sensitive. Having a specific time frame in mind will enable us to change a habit or develop a new habit rather than just "hope" to do so. If you don't give a goal a definite time frame, it will probably not happen. You have to decide when you will start working on the goal and when you plan to complete it. Goals can always be revised due to unexpected events, our level of maturity, the knowledge we gain, the opportunities that come to us, and the actual rate of our progress.

PRESS BEYOND THE INITIAL DISCOMFORT AND PAIN

In order to maintain the process of change while building the new habit or discarding the old one, we need to press beyond the initial discomfort and pain. This becomes easier over time. Most people don't realize that when seeking change, there's often a threshold of discomfort to get beyond in order to obtain victory. Unfortunately, many individuals are kept to a lower level in life because they give up too soon. They may be emotionally or physically tired and therefore fail to press on. We have to give it our all on our first wind because there's a second wind in us, but we don't get to the second wind unless we exhaust ourselves using the first one.

It is often the case that we won't grow beyond the level of pain that we're willing to tolerate. We must get to the point where we can say, "I know it's uncomfortable for me to (get up earlier, work longer, keep experimenting to find a solution), but I'm willing to bear the discomfort." When we have great passion for a purpose or goal, we give it everything we have, even to the point where we are about to quit. And right at that point is where we often get that second wind.

Usually, the hardest part of the journey is when you're in first gear and struggling up the hill. When you shift into second, it gets a little easier; when you get into third, you start coasting; and when you get into fourth, you're really in a cruising zone. Don't quit while you're only in first gear!

THE HARDEST PART OF THE JOURNEY IS
WHEN YOU'RE IN FIRST GEAR.
IT GETS EASIER AS YOU GAIN MOMENTUM.

FOCUS ON THE REWARDS

Similarly, in the midst of change, it is easy to want to fall back into old, negative patterns. But we must look beyond self-gratification and immediate pleasure. For instance, if you are building a business, you will have to make certain sacrifices of your time. There will always be opportunities to spend time on secondary things. Those other things aren't necessarily wrong, but if you do them, you may not reach your goal. Or, suppose you are on your second week of an exercise program and your muscles ache and you'd rather sit down and watch TV than go for a brisk walk. You have to keep in mind the rewards of a healthier and trimmer body to stay motivated.

Always remember to focus on the result of your diligence. List the benefits of breaking the negative habit or establishing the positive practice. It may be the reward of prosperous business established, a healthier body, a more organized life, a new skill learned, an educational degree earned, or a project completed. Ask yourself, "If I stick with this, what will happen?" Then ask yourself, "If I *don't* stick with this, what will happen?"

STARVE THE BAD HABIT

In essence, when we want to break a bad habit, we need to "starve it out." For example, my wife had an "addiction" to chocolate, so she stayed away from chocolate for a solid year. Some habits are a matter of degrees. It's not that she never ate chocolate again, but she broke the habit's grip so that it didn't control her attitudes or behavior or cause her to overdo it.

To paraphrase a well-known proverb, overcoming negative habits are, to a large extent, the result of resisting temptation. Temptation is a provocation to do or to be something outside your character or belief system. But temptation is temporary, which means if we can get past it, we can avoid succumbing to it. I take encouragement from this statement from the New Testament writer Paul: "No temptation has overtaken you except such as is common to man; but God is faithful, who will not allow you to be tempted beyond what you are able, but with the temptation will also make the way of escape, that you may be able to bear it."[20]

We don't want to become dominated by what is called the "pleasure principle," continuing to indulge in something just because it feels good, while allowing it to harm us or impede our progress. To use a simple

20. 1 Corinthians 10:13.

example, to overcome the habit of sleeping too late, we first have to resist the temptation to push the snooze button and go back to sleep! We starve that negative habit by getting up as soon as the alarm goes off and having a good start on our day.

Remember, you are always going to face temptations to stray off course. So when you get ready to break a negative practice or to establish a winning practice in your life, expect to be tempted to do the opposite. One of temptation's most powerful weapons is surprise. We weren't ready for it when it showed up. We didn't anticipate it drawing us away from our plan or goal. So learn to expect temptation and keep alert for surprise attacks. Commit ahead of time to resist any temptation that works against your purpose. We have to maintain our desire for change and our determination to see the process through, recognizing that temptation is only temporary.

TEMPTATION IS A PROVOCATION TO DO OR TO BE SOMETHING OUTSIDE YOUR CHARACTER OR BELIEF SYSTEM.

REPLACE THE BAD HABIT WITH A GOOD ONE

As I mentioned earlier, to break a negative habit, we often need to exchange a bad practice for a good one, or a neutral one. For example, when some people are in the process of quitting smoking, they chew gum as a substitute until they overcome their addiction to nicotine.

We can be more successful at making this exchange of practices by reminding ourselves that our negative habit may be driven by unresolved issues in our life. Whenever we experience stress, frustration, confusion, or anxiety, we might be strongly tempted to go back to a negative habit or addiction because it has an anesthetizing or soothing effect on us. It may calm us down temporarily, but it just dulls or distracts our feelings rather than resolving them. It goes back to how habits are formed and the powerful influence of our feelings. It's essential to determine ahead of time what positive responses we will make when we feel stress and anxiety. Rather than indulge in bad feelings and give in to the negative habit, we can choose to take a walk, call a friend, pray, read an inspirational article, or do something else constructive and uplifting. Additionally, our bad habits may come from spending time with those who practice the same bad habits. We need to keep in mind that to change a bad habit, we may have to change some of our associations, a topic we will explore further in coming chapters.

ENLIST THE HELP OF OTHERS

Don't try to do form a new habit alone. An incredible advantage comes into your life when you get just one other person to help you or encourage you. I heard about an interesting experiment that supports this idea. Researchers had people put their bare feet into ice water to see how long they could stand it. They couldn't endure it for very long. But then the researchers brought in a friend for each person to encourage them while their feet were in the ice water. Every participant was able to keep their feet in the water at least twice as long with the encouragement and presence of a friend than they could by themselves.

When we align with others in any endeavor, the results usually increase and can even be exponential. This is why it is wise to have a friend or mentor support you when you are developing a new habit. Similarly, when dismantling a bad habit, it is often helpful to find a role model, someone you can connect with, who has successfully accomplished what you desire to do. We can often feel like an oddball, as if we're the only one struggling with a particular problem. Regardless of what we are dealing with, others have faced the same thing or something similar. We can be inspired by hope when we learn how somebody else has overcome it. A role model doesn't have to be someone we know personally; it might be someone whom we read about in a book or follow on an Internet blog. And remember, whether or not they have gone through the same experience, sometimes it's enough just to have a friend by our side, as we saw in the experiment with the ice water.

Whenever I need to break a negative habit or build a positive habit, I turn to God as my greatest Friend and support. I ask Him daily for help, saying, "God, I know I can't do this by myself. I need Your strength and Your wisdom so that when I'm weak, You'll be strong in me. Help me not go back to this old habit, and help me to persevere in developing this new habit." Our Creator has built us to succeed; we are engineered for excellence, and we can rely on His help.

MAKE IT FUN

Whenever you dismantle an old habit or develop a new habit, don't allow the process to become mundane and boring. Find a way to bring joy and fun into it. Years ago, I worked in the Bronner Brothers warehouse, and there were times when we'd have huge shipments coming in, and we would have many rollers and boxes to unload off the truck. It was hard work, but we'd be whistling and singing, and it made things go easier and faster. There are simple but effective ways to bring enjoyment into the process of breaking bad habits and cultivating positive habits. Be creative with it.

RECORD AND CELEBRATE YOUR PROGRESS

Change rarely happens overnight. Since it takes time to develop new habits, it's helpful to record your progress according to the goals you have set. You might keep a brief log of your advancement or improvement, or write your thoughts and feelings in a journal as you go through the process. For example, it could be helpful to record how you felt when you temporarily went back to your bad habit and how you were able to get back on track. Or how it felt when you successfully resisted the urge to give up.

As you measure your progress, reward your improvement, no matter how small. Find a way to celebrate your victories, even if it's merely putting a check mark on your calendar for each day you work toward your goal. It's always encouraging to be able to say, "I've had another successful (week, month) at (building this business, improving this relationship, making progress on this project, exercising regularly)." Mark major milestones along the way as you develop your habit.

MAKE A "NO EXCEPTIONS" POLICY

Author and speaker Jim Rohn said, "Motivation is what gets you started. Habit is what keeps you going." Once you have established a habit, stick to your decision and maintain the change through consistency. There will always be a temptation to say to yourself, *Look how far you've come. Just let it slide this one time.* However, make a "no exceptions" policy. The more you resist dropping a new habit or going back to an old habit, the stronger you will become. The more you yield, the weaker you will become.

Additionally, an old habit will sometime resurface even after you thought it was completely conquered. Don't allow that to discourage you. Every relapse is an opportunity to reassess where you are, improve, and grow. It's never too late to change or to renew your commitment to change.

A PLEASURE AND A DELIGHT

Let's not kid ourselves—breaking an old habit or developing a new one can be challenging. But the above guidelines will help you to establish winning practices in your life. You can build positive habits that will benefit not only yourself but also those in your household, place of employment, community, and nation. When you start off, it will seem like hard work, but if you persevere, the results and even the process will become a pleasure and a delight.

"BAD HABITS ARE EASIER TO ABANDON TODAY
THAN TOMORROW."

BENEFITS OF A WISDOM-DRIVEN LIFE

* Dismantling negative habits and developing positive habits supports our endeavors to fulfill our purpose in life.

* When we change our habits, we change our destiny.

+ Setting goals enables us to progressively achieve success.

+ Building positive habits can benefit not only ourselves but also those in our household, place of employment, community, and nation.

APPLYING WISDOM

1. Take inventory of your life according to the guideline in this chapter. What are your strengths and weaknesses? Determine in which areas you need to break negative habits and develop positive habits.

2. Choose a small habit to dismantle or to develop, and begin following the steps to change.

3. Record your progress, celebrating your accomplishments, both small and large.

7

WISDOM DEVELOPS KEY RELATIONSHIPS, PART 1: THE POWER OF INFLUENCE

Those who influence us most project what our future will be.

In addition to our daily habits, the quality of our relationships contributes significantly to our success or failure. Depending on which people we choose to spend time with, our life can be heaven—or hell—on earth. I'm not just referring to making a wise decision about choosing a spouse, as essential as that is. I'm talking about using wisdom concerning the whole range of our relationships, including our friends, partners, associates, mentors, fellow members of organizations, advisors, and other involvements and connections.

You probably know some children who never met a stranger—they'll walk up to anyone because they're friendly by nature. This innocent quality is positive in many ways, but it can also have a negative side because it puts them at risk from people whose motivations are far from good. Likewise, we cannot afford to be indiscriminate in our relationships. Often, those whose life has taken a downward spiral can trace it back to someone in their life who led them down a wasteful or destructive path—someone who, in hindsight, they wish they had never gotten involved with. Conversely, those whose life has improved in significant ways can generally trace it back to someone in their life who lifted them up and showed them what they could become.

> THE QUALITY OF OUR RELATIONSHIPS
> MAKES A SIGNIFICANT DIFFERENCE TO
> OUR SUCCESS OR FAILURE.

"THE LAW OF THE INNER CIRCLE"

"The law of the inner circle," which John Maxwell describes in his book *The 21 Irrefutable Laws of Leadership*, says that those who are closest to you determine your level of success. Maxwell reminds us that there are four kinds of people in the world: those who add to us, those who subtract from us, those who multiply us, and those who divide us. We need to draw close to individuals who add to us and multiply us while pulling back from individuals who subtract from us and divide us.

We must carefully consider these ideas because we will begin to move in the direction of the people whose company we keep. What kind of company are you keeping? In addition to your immediate family, picture your close friends, associates, and advisors who have the greatest influence on you. Think about where they are in life or where they are going, because they may well be projecting your own future. You can tell the intent or purpose of something based on the path it begins to move you along in life. Does your association with these individuals cause you to go up or down, forward or backward? Are the relationships positive or negative? Before you commit to a relationship or an association, you need to ask yourself, *Where is this person going, and is that destination a place I honestly want to go?*

BEWARE OF MIXED ASSOCIATIONS

If you frequently find yourself taking two steps forward and one step backward in life, it may be that your associations are mixed—some of your relationships are positive and move you forward, but others are negative and cause you to have setbacks. As soon as you make headway in one area, you end up being pulled back in another. It seems as if you can never get ahead. We can't fulfill our calling if we have mixed associations. Our success will be divided and limited.

Some people focus merely on superficialities. But the people who are the most fulfilled, as well as the happiest and healthiest to be around, are those who give themselves to a purpose. If you are not as committed to your purpose as you used to be, and your motivations have become more selfish, that's often a sign you have allowed mixed associations into your life. Beware of those who begin to rob you of your identity.

THERE ARE FOUR KINDS OF PEOPLE IN THE WORLD: THOSE WHO ADD TO US, THOSE WHO SUBTRACT FROM US, THOSE WHO MULTIPLY US, AND THOSE WHO DIVIDE US.

We can move to a higher level of life when we associate with people who live intentionally—who live their lives on purpose, with purpose, and for purpose. When such people have an influence in our life, we become more focused on our own calling and less self-centered. We stop considering "What's in it for me?" or "How much am I going to make?" but rather "What's best for my (family, organization, committee)? How can we all thrive and succeed together?" If it's always just about us, we'll never be able to come into that wonderful place of understanding and living according to purpose.

There may be times when we can't avoid close contact with someone who has a negative influence on us; in those instances, we have to take special care to keep focused on our purpose, goals, and principles. Seek to cultivate the right kind of influences in your life and to choose the right company. If someone can walk out of your life without being missed, it means they were unaligned with your purpose. But when somebody can encourage you in your purpose and cause you to progress in it, that relationship can take you a long way.

WE MOVE TO A HIGHER LEVEL WHEN WE ASSOCIATE WITH PEOPLE WHO LIVE INTENTIONALLY—WHO LIVE THEIR LIVES ON PURPOSE, WITH PURPOSE, AND FOR PURPOSE.

RECOGNIZING UNHEALTHY RELATIONSHIPS

We often tolerate unhelpful and unhealthy relationships in our lives because we don't stop to consider the effect they are having on us. Here are some guidelines for recognizing those who are having a negative influence on your life.

PEOPLE WHO DRAIN YOU

Have you ever sent someone's phone call directly to voicemail because you cringed when you saw their number flash on the screen of your phone? You think, *I just don't have the energy to talk to them right now!* There are certain people you never hear from until they need something. When they call, something inside you says, *Okay, I know they want something. I wonder what it will be this time.* Usually, what they're asking for is not related to either their purpose or yours but rather to some way they can use you. Don't allow people to drain you of your energy or other resources. Keep such people at bay.

PEOPLE WHO DELAY YOU

There are people who will monopolize your life if you let them. Time is a precious commodity. You only have so much of it. The older you get, the more you become aware of this fact. You feel that time is speeding on while your life is winding down. Those who don't understand your purpose and are not helping to propel you toward it can delay you. For example, you'll be on track to do something, when someone calls with another so-called "emergency." They don't care what your schedule is like or what you're committed to doing. Legitimate concerns and emergencies are one thing, but we have to be careful not to let people delay us from fulfilling our purpose and goals in life for extraneous reasons.

PEOPLE WHO DISTRACT YOU

Certain people can distract you by urging you to become involved in less important matters so that your priorities and goals get thrown off, and your plans are slowed down. Their motivations may not be bad, but spending time with them or doing things for them would not be the best use of your time. You've heard the saying that some things are good for us, some things are better, but certain things are best? That's a good way to decide whether you are being distracted from your purpose. Ask yourself, *Is this relationship or activity one of the "best" things to include in my life? Or is it "good" or "better" and thus secondary?*

PEOPLE WHO DECEIVE YOU

Sometimes, you don't really know someone until you have a little experience in dealing with them; then you understand their true motivations. Things are not always as they seem. You might not immediately like someone but later come to respect them for their good character and generous nature. Or, you might think someone is a pleasant person but then recognize they are actually manipulative of others, deceiving them for their own advantage. Some people may come into your life and purposely present themselves one way, but then turn out to be something quite different. For example, you think they are just being friendly toward you, until you discover they have been showboating, exaggerating, trying to impress you, because they are deeply in debt and want to get money from you. You can be deceived in any relationship, so exercise discernment and wisdom.

PEOPLE WHO DERAIL YOU

We've noted that some people steer us off course simply because they are self-absorbed or thoughtless of our time. But with others, the influence is more threatening because they actively tempt us to do things that go against our conscience or cause us to lapse from following our purpose. Beware of those who seek to get you to do something against your beliefs and character.

DEVELOP A FILTERING SYSTEM

For each of our relationships, therefore, we need to determine what degree of proximity or distance we should have with them. It's important to establish a filtering system so that we don't allow just anybody and everybody to have a strong influence in our lives. First, we need to eliminate time with those who have proven to have a negative or even damaging effect on us (or at least reduce that time if contact cannot be completely avoided). Second, we need to limit our time with certain others, not because they're terrible people, not because of any character flaws or because it would be personally damaging to spend time with them, but because their goals or interests don't align with ours, and they would be distracting to our purpose. With people in this second group, we should obviously still want the best for them, and we might spend time with them on occasion—they just can't be among our close friends and associates.

To use a financial analogy, you don't put assets where liabilities go, or liabilities where assets go. There's a place for each, but they need to be positioned correctly. And you cannot afford too many liabilities, or you're going to bankrupt yourself.

I'm not suggesting we interact with people only for what we can receive from them. Far from it. True purpose always involves uplifting others and helping them. What I am saying is that we must seriously consider whom we allow to impact the course of our lives.

As you develop a relationship filtering system, you can use the following key questions to evaluate the effect other people are having on you and to determine whether they are an asset or a liability:

+ Does this individual support my purpose, or do they cause me to be double-minded about it and to be diverted from my calling?

+ Has this person encouraged my dream or are they a dream-killer?

+ Does this individual encourage genuine, significant, positive relationships in my life, or do they draw me away from them?

+ Is this individual sincere in their friendship or just trying to tickle my ego so they can use me?

+ Is this person a constructive influence in my personal, professional, emotional, or intellectual growth, or an encumbering one?

+ Does this individual motivate me to do what is right or try to intimidate me into doing what is wrong?

+ Am I a better person or a worse person as a result of having this individual in my life?

Finally, a factor that is especially important to me:

+ Has my relationship with God been strengthened or weakened since this person has been in my life?

In the next chapter, we will explore the positive side of key relationships: the types of people with whom we all need to develop and maintain purposeful ties.

BENEFITS OF A WISDOM-DRIVEN LIFE

+ We move to a higher level of life when we associate with people who live intentionally—who live their lives on purpose, with purpose, and for purpose.

+ When positive people influence our life, we are more focused on our calling and we become a better person.

+ When we establish a filtering system for our relationships, we can choose who will have a strong influence in our life.

APPLYING WISDOM

1. Begin to assess the various relationships in your life according to the filtering system guidelines in this chapter and determine whether they are assets or liabilities to you.

2. What relationships have you been tolerating or even giving high priority to that are actually detrimental to you?

3. Make a specific decision to eliminate or reduce time with friends and associates who drain, delay, distract, deceive, or derail you. Develop a concrete plan to follow-up with that decision.

8

WISDOM DEVELOPS KEY RELATIONSHIPS, PART 2: CULTIVATING LIFE INFLUENCES

"Walk with the wise and become wise."[21]

We all need people who can guide us in wise living and encourage us to follow our principles and continue to pursue our calling. The positive influences in our life will generally come under four main categories. First, there are those in proximity to us who believe in us and support us in the various facets of our lives. Those in this group might be our spouse, parents, siblings, other family members, friends, mentors, and employers. Second, there are those who do not live near us but are still rooting for us; they believe in us, pray for us, and support us from a distance in other ways. Third, there are those whom we have never personally met but who inspire us and teach us by their words or actions, or both. Finally, there is the Great One, the Creator, who is always with us and for us, ready to provide guidance and help on the wisdom journey. Each has a part in helping us live a successful life.

21. Proverbs 13:20 (NIV).

KEY RELATIONSHIPS TO CULTIVATE

Proverbs says that "in the multitude of counselors there is safety."[22] The following are key relationships that everyone needs but that we must make a point to develop and maintain. (Some of these relationships may overlap, with one person having more than one role in our life.)

SOMEONE WHO CAN RELATE TO US

First, we need someone who has the ability to relate to us, who understands our purpose and the place where we currently are in life—mentally, emotionally, physically, and spiritually. An excellent definition of a best friend is a person who brings out the best in you. They know everything there is to know about you, and they love you anyway. We can't do extraordinary things in fulfillment of our vision if we're surrounded by people who don't believe in us and what we can do. As we discussed in the previous chapter, whenever we wonder if a certain relationship is healthy for us, we can ask ourselves this central question: "Am I closer to my purpose as a result of this relationship, or am I driven further away by it?" When we're committed to our purpose, we allow our close relationships to be derived from that purpose. We need to position ourselves with those who understand, support, or share our vision. This is one of the reasons why people's close friends are often among those who are in the same profession. Their fellowship is derived from their shared purpose.

My wife has helped to align me closer to my purpose, and I've helped to align her closer to hers. Our coming together in marriage was confirmed by our respective purposes. If, when we were dating, she had pulled me away from what I was meant to do, I would have known that it was a wrong relationship for me. But I am grateful to God for His grace in allowing me to meet and connect with someone who understood my purpose and has helped to propel me toward it.

SOMEONE WHO CAN CORRECT US

We also need someone to whom we voluntarily make ourselves accountable, someone who can speak the truth to us and point out where

---

22. Proverbs 11:14; see also Proverbs 24:6.

we are deviating from the path of our purpose and from a lifestyle of wisdom. To have such a relationship, we must develop the quality of teachableness—being able to receive constructive criticism and correction and to accept good counsel. This isn't always easy for us, but it is essential to our success. When we were young, our parents and other adults filled this role in our lives. As adults, we don't need the same form of correction; but as I emphasized earlier, we all have blind spots and areas where we need improvement. We have to make provision for personal, professional, and relational growth by entering into an arrangement of accountability with someone trustworthy who has our best interests in mind.

If you don't have anyone who can point out to you when you are doing something wrong, it means that no one has the ability to put you back on the right course when you deviate from it. Some people make themselves accountable to their spouse in this way, but not everyone is comfortable with that. They feel it may hinder the relationship, and they prefer someone outside the marriage to fill this role. Every person is different, so decide whom you feel you can be accountable to and allow them to keep you on track.

SOMEONE WHO CAN ASSIST IN OUR DEVELOPMENT

Additionally, we need people who can help direct us and develop us, depositing their wisdom, instruction, experiences, and skills into our life so that we can build on them. Make sure that you surround yourself with people who have the ability to make such investments in you, such as an older relative, a friend, a teacher, an employer, a businessperson, a clergyperson, or a community leader. An excellent definition of a mentor is one who does things *for us*, then *with us*, and then watches us do them *on our own* in the course of our development.

SOMEONE WHO CAN DEFEND US

Furthermore, we need individuals in our life who will defend us when we face opposition or potential harm. Again, when we are young, our parents and other relatives should do this for us. Later, if we marry, our spouse is intended to be the primary person in that role. Another relative, a good friend, or a mentor can also serve as a strong defender in our lives. When someone tries to take advantage of us, then our "defender" will step in and say, in effect, "Wait just a moment—that's *not* going to happen," and will thwart the other person's bad intentions toward us. A defender might also make an appeal on our behalf or give us access to others who can help us advance in a specific way, such as gain further education or obtain a job.

SOMEONE WHO CAN TEACH US TO DREAM

We all need someone who can teach us to dream, or our lives are in danger of becoming mediocre. This is the person who can inspire you to have a vision that's bigger than what you can afford, and bigger than the personnel and resources you already have, so you can reach farther than you ever expected. I'm glad that I grew up in a house where my father was a dreamer, and I'm glad God brought others into my life who were visionaries, so I could learn to dream, too. I wouldn't be where I am today without them. Some people were raised in households where they were never exposed to anyone who taught them how to dream. If that has been your situation, seek out those who can fill that role for you now.

SOMEONE WHO CAN TEACH US TO DARE

Every dream has to be accompanied by a certain amount of daring—audacious faith, courage, and boldness. We have to learn to dare because, as we have seen, if our dream does not intimidate us in some way, if it doesn't cost more than we currently have available to pay for it, and if it is something we can achieve all on our own, it probably is not big enough.

I've known some daring individuals who were willing to lose everything they had in order to invest in what they believed in and live their dream. I also know people who have dreams but don't have enough courage to go after them because they think things like, *What if I fail? What if it doesn't work? What if I run out of money? What if they don't like what I have to offer?* You just have to arrive at a point of faith where you give your dream everything you've got.

I've visited many people on their deathbed, and no one ever told me about all the things they had done that they regretted. Rather, I've often heard people talk about regretting the things they never had the courage to do and couldn't do anything about now. Following a true vision takes daring, and you need people in your life who can model what it is like to take risks and to try things—even if they might not make it all the way.

YOU HAVE TO ARRIVE AT A POINT WHERE YOU GIVE YOUR DREAM EVERYTHING YOU'VE GOT.

SOMEONE WHO CAN PROVIDE NEEDED RESOURCES

There are some people in this world who have tremendous resources, including money and other assets. Since our dream is bigger than our resources, we're going to need such people in our lives to help us fulfill our calling. I'm not saying we should expect a free ride from them. Instead, we should make a practice of investing in their lives and serving them, as well as others, while preparing for our purpose. I encourage you to find a need and serve that need with an open heart.

On one occasion, I took a businessman in our church out to lunch and told him I wanted to share some things that would help his business. I never asked for a dime. But at the end of the lunch, he took out his checkbook and wrote out a check for two hundred fifty thousand dollars. Of course, I said, "Let's have lunch again next week!"

Another time, I was invited to attend a meeting in Atlanta where a billionaire was speaking to a select group of two hundred people. It was in a banquet environment in a nice hotel, and when I arrived, I was seated at the head table near the billionaire.

As I sat there, I silently asked God to show me a need in this man's life that I could meet. You may ask, "What needs could a billionaire possibly have?" Every person, no matter how wealthy, has needs in their life, because money does not solve everything. And if we always look for the big things, we can miss what God wants to do through a very simple thing.

After the billionaire finished his meal, he asked for a cup of coffee. And in that fine hotel, they brought him piping-hot coffee—in a paper cup. I saw he was having difficulty drinking his coffee because the hot liquid was burning his fingers through the cup, and I immediately recognized his need. At first, I said to myself, *I don't work here; it's not my job to serve.* But I had noticed the problem, so I got up and found a ceramic cup, brought it back to the table, took the paper cup of hot coffee, and poured it into the ceramic cup. When I did that, the man looked up at me, pointed to the empty chair next to him, and said, "*Sit down.*"

I never would have gotten an invitation to sit next to a billionaire if I hadn't noticed an immediate need in his life, however small it was, and had enough humility to look past the potential awkwardness of the situation to serve him. For the next fifteen to twenty minutes, this man opened his heart and talked to me as if I was his own son, sharing information that would have cost me hundreds of thousands of dollars in professional consulting. I believe that if you make a practice of serving others, even those who initially don't seem to need anything, your own needs will be met.

SOMEONE WHO CAN RESTORE OUR CONFIDENCE

Sometimes, we make bad choices that cause us to stumble in life; other times we undergo difficult circumstances, through no fault of our own, that cause us to lose our footing. When we make mistakes or face setbacks, we can feel we're no longer worthy or capable of pursuing our purpose. We just want to give up. As a result, we may withdraw from other people and withdraw into ourselves.

During such times, a strong supporter in our life can help awaken us from our dormant state and restore our confidence, encouraging us, "Don't give up on your dream. You can still make it work. It has great potential. *You* have great potential." They can help us to develop a mind-set that says, "My career is not dead; it's able to be recovered," or "My talent is not lost; it's able to be restored." If we have a purpose within us that keeps bubbling up, and if we have a determined person inside of us, we may stumble, but we can regain our balance. We can bring back the person of purpose we once were. And one of the best ways to ensure this is to have established key people in our life who believe in us and can help us recover our conviction and confidence.

SOMEONE WHO CAN SHOW US HOW TO DIE WELL

Yes, you read that correctly. Knowing how to die well is an essential part of the wisdom-driven life. Why? Because how you finish in life matters more than how you start in life. We don't determine the way we are born, and we can't predict *when* or *how* we will die, but we can determine *the way* we will die. And we need role models who can show us the right way to die.

I'm glad I've lived long enough to have experienced vital relationships with remarkable mentors who have since passed on—relationships that have been some of the most significant of my life. While I learned much from my mentors during their lives, I have also seen many of them on their deathbeds approaching the end without fear or trepidation but with peace and courage. I have also observed many people of faith who have looked death in the face and been exuberant and full of joy even as cancer or another illness ravaged their bodies. They have taught me how to die well.

HOW YOU FINISH IN LIFE MATTERS MORE
THAN HOW YOU START.

One of my greatest mentors was dying of cancer. He was at the end of his life, but he didn't go through a roll call of all of his accomplishments. He didn't talk about any of the properties he owned or about the money he had in the bank or about the educational degrees he had earned, although all of these were impressive. Neither did he have any fear or regrets. The only thing he talked about was the quality of his relationships, and he expressed to me over and over, "I love you." His life wasn't about things or achievements. He left a legacy of love and investment in others.

What good is it to be successful in life if you don't know how to die well? Death is part of the process of life. I don't believe death is an end but a beginning. It's a commencement into another dimension of life. So, find key role models who can show you not only how to live well but also how to die well.

BRINGING OUT THE BEST IN US

Those with whom we cultivate key relationships have the ability to promote positive qualities and gifts within us as they continually point us toward our purpose. They help us to grow through our life experiences, and they support us in many different ways, including by giving us wise counsel. As Solomon said, "Walk with the wise and become wise."

I believe the answer to every problem is a person. I'm very grateful for the various people who have come into my life at critical points and taught me the wisdom and knowledge I needed. Some people will come into our life for just a short time but will lift us to another level of growth or achievement by their inspiration, example, or knowledge. Others will be in our life for a certain season to fulfill various needs, and then it will be time for them—or us—to move on. And there are certain people with whom we will have longstanding relationships and who will make extensive contributions to our lives. Regardless of how long they are with us, we can cultivate relationships with key individuals who will develop, challenge, and motivate us in the ways we've discussed in this chapter. Let us seek out these positive influencers who will believe in us and always bring out the best in us.

BENEFITS OF A WISDOM-DRIVEN LIFE

+ Purposely cultivating relationships with significant people as positive influencers in our life will lift us to a higher level of growth, achievement, and fulfillment.

+ We will move closer to fulfilling our purpose as we establish key relationships with people who can relate to us, correct us, assist in our development, defend us, teach us to dream, teach us to dare, provide needed resources, restore our confidence, and show us how to die well.

APPLYING WISDOM

1. List specific people in your life who fill the various key relationships described in this chapter and how they function in those roles.

2. Are you missing any key relationships? Whom do you know who might fill those roles? Make a plan for cultivating key relationships in those areas.

9

WISDOM TEACHES YOUR DOLLARS SOME SENSE, PART 1: AN ENVIRONMENT FOR GROWTH AND ABUNDANCE

Money helps us to pursue our purpose in life, and building
wealth broadens our options and reach in fulfilling that purpose.

MONEY MATTERS

In my experience, there are two groups of people to whom it's not always
easy to talk about money—those who have a lot of money, and those
who have little money. Perhaps the first group thinks they already know all
they need to know about finances, and the second group doesn't think the
information applies to them or ever will. But if people understood the true
purpose of money and having financial resources, almost everyone would
want to hear more about it and how it works!

I have also found that many people think about the role of money in
either limiting or unsound ways. Certain people place too much emphasis

on making money, elevating it to their primary goal in life; others place too little emphasis on making money, criticizing and even rejecting the idea. Many people of faith seem to misunderstand the role and value of money because they misread a statement by the New Testament writer Paul. Consequently, they have come to view money as a corrupt thing, emphasizing, "Money is the root of all evil!" They don't realize that Paul actually wrote, "For the *love of* money is the root of all evil."[23] We don't have to choose between God and money; we only have to choose which one we are going to serve.[24]

In other words, it's okay to have riches, but it's not okay for riches to have us. Again, when people have an inordinate love of money, they prioritize it above more important and valuable things, sometimes to the point that it consumes them. That mind-set is a root of all kinds of negative and damaging things. We're meant to love people and use money. But when their priorities are off, many people do the opposite: they love money and use people—usually in order to get more money.

Solomon, who was not only the wisest man who ever lived but also the richest king of his day, wrote, "He who loves silver will not be satisfied with silver; nor he who loves abundance, with increase. This also is vanity."[25] Whoever loves money will never be satisfied with increase because they will never feel they have enough. And while they may accrue more and more wealth, it won't make them any happier.

People can develop a love of money by believing that "money is power." They think that the more money they get, the more power and influence they will have, so money becomes the thing they live for. It's true that they may be able to buy a certain amount of power and influence with their money, but they will inevitably use that power and influence for the wrong reasons and in misapplied ways.

Thus, having wealth doesn't guarantee that we will use it well. Even if some people were to obtain their desire of becoming rich, they probably wouldn't hold on to their money for very long. Most people who win the lottery end up mishandling the money and becoming worse off financially

23. 1 Timothy 6:10 (KJV).
24. See, for example, Matthew 6:24.
25. Ecclesiastes 5:10.

(and otherwise) than they were previously. Having an abundance of wealth didn't automatically make them good money managers. The principle is that if you don't know how to handle the money you have now, you won't know how to handle any additional money you may receive. This usually happens because most people's desires rise to the level of their income. Regardless of how much money they might have coming in, they will remain at the same income-debt ratio. As we saw in the chapters on habits, our lives will not change for the better until we change our negative practices.

HAVING A CLEAR UNDERSTANDING OF THE PURPOSE AND ROLE OF MONEY ENABLES US TO EMPLOY THE PRACTICAL TOOLS RELATED TO BUILDING WEALTH FOR THE RIGHT REASONS AND WITH THE BEST RESULTS.

One time, when Jesus was teaching a large crowd, a man called out to Him, asking Him to arbitrate in a dispute; he wanted the Teacher to make his brother divide the family inheritance with him. Jesus first replied to the man that it wasn't His job to settle his dispute with his brother. Then, perhaps sensing the man's motive, he told the crowd, "Take heed and beware of covetousness, for one's life does not consist in the abundance of the things he possesses."[26] Whether or not the brother was in the wrong was not the real issue. It was how the man in the crowd viewed the value of possessions in his own life. He needed to grasp that the essence of his life did not consist in what he owned, nor in having an abundance of material goods.

Again, there's nothing wrong with material prosperity or making money; it's how we view money that can cause us problems, and it's what we do with it that matters. That's why it's essential to have a clear understanding of the true purpose and role of money that can guide us in using it wisely,

---

26. Luke 12:15.

no matter how much or how little of it we may have at a given time. Only when we have this perspective can we employ all the practical tools related to making and investing money for the right reasons, in the most beneficial context, and with the best results. I highlight a number of those practical tools in the next chapter. But first, what is the reason for having money and other material resources?

THE OBJECT OF MONEY

Of course, we all need a certain amount of money and resources to provide housing, food, and other necessities of life for ourselves and our families. That is a primary responsibility. Money also enables us to improve our lives, for example by allowing us to pay for a college education; or to enjoy life, such as making it possible for us to pay for a family vacation.

Yet here is the deeper reason for having and utilizing financial resources: money helps us to pursue our purpose in life, and building wealth broadens our options and reach in fulfilling that purpose. Thus, making, saving, and investing money are integral components of living our lives according to our calling. As I've expressed previously, all the resources we need to complete our purpose will ultimately come to us as we follow our calling, and that includes financial resources. Although, as we have seen, some of those resources may be provided by others who have great financial means, a certain amount of it will come from us.

The way we manage our money is therefore significant to our purpose. For example, if we are continually in debt, how can we invest in our dreams for ourselves and our families? How can we be ready for various opportunities that would be open to us if we only had the funds? The reason many people haven't been able to manifest their personal vision or dream is that they have been hindered by a lack of money. For example, they may have needed people with other skills to help them but had no funds to hire anyone. Therefore, instead of merely thinking about how we can get money and spend it, as many people do, we should think about how we can generate it and invest it in our purpose so that we and others can live meaningful and prosperous lives.

FRUITFUL, PRODUCTIVE, AND PROFITABLE

In order to build wealth, we must realize that we are designed with the potential to be fruitful, productive, and profitable. We just need to gain the knowledge that will enable us to enter into that capability. I believe the book of Genesis reveals something strategic about this point. After describing the creation of the world, including humanity, it says that God commissioned human beings as caretakers of a garden, or an environment, in which everything around them was growing and producing.[27] They couldn't look in any direction and not see fruitfulness, productivity, and beauty. This was the environment over which they were given stewardship, or management responsibilities. In a sense, this atmosphere was speaking to them not only about their role as earth's caretakers but also about their own potential as "co-creators"—it was a reflection of the great possibilities for fruitfulness and creativity and productivity contained within them.[28] This purpose for humanity has not changed.

HUMAN BEINGS WERE CREATED WITH
THE POTENTIAL TO BE FRUITFUL, PRODUCTIVE,
AND PROFITABLE ACCORDING TO THEIR PURPOSE.

So let me ask you: when you look around you or within you, do you see the potential for fruitfulness? We know that this earth we live in has many problems, but it is still a place where things are—or can be—productive, fruitful, and profitable. We know that our lives are less than perfect, but we are still people who are—or can be—productive, fruitful, and profitable. That is why, when we apply wisdom and knowledge to our finances, we can cultivate an environment that will yield growth and abundance.

---

27. See Genesis 1–2.
28. See Genesis 1:28.

WHAT IS TRUE PROSPERITY?

As we seek to build material wealth and manage our finances, we should always remember that prosperity is far broader than money. True prosperity refers not only to monetary abundance but also to wholeness of body, mind, and spirit. It's about having solid relationships. It's about living in congruity with your inner core values. We're not prosperous if we scheme and cheat, and then have to take a pill to sleep at night and another pill to get up in the morning. We're not prosperous if we're focused mainly on how much money we have or if we are self-absorbed and live in isolation from other people. Prosperity is about doing what we were born to do and loving life.

Ultimately, nobody else can tell you what it means for you to be prosperous. Why? Because, as we have seen, true prosperity means fulfilling your unique, God-given purpose. What you need for your calling will be different from what someone else needs for their calling. Prosperity therefore has individual expressions, but it is always for blessing—blessing for ourselves and blessing for others through the life we've been called to lead and to share with others.

"WEALTH CONSISTS NOT IN HAVING GREAT POSSESSIONS, BUT IN HAVING FEW WANTS."
—EPICTETUS

BENEFITS OF A WISDOM-DRIVEN LIFE

+ Money helps us to pursue our purpose in life, and building wealth broadens our options and reach in fulfilling that purpose.

+ Applying wisdom and knowledge to our finances enables us to cultivate an environment that yields growth and abundance.

+   Prosperity expresses itself in our lives in individual ways according to our purpose, but it is always for blessing—not only for ourselves but also for others.

APPLYING WISDOM

1. What has been your general attitude toward money? Have you leaned more toward seeing money as your primary focus in life or as an evil that corrupts?

2. What would you do with the money if you suddenly came into great wealth?

3. Has your perspective toward money changed at all after reading this chapter? If so, in what ways?

4. How might you refocus your current finances toward fulfilling your purpose in life?

10

WISDOM TEACHES YOUR DOLLARS SOME SENSE, PART 2: PROVEN FINANCIAL STRATEGIES

"Wealth flows from energy and ideas."
—William Feather

You don't need an MBA from Harvard to understand money and manage it well. The following are practical, proven strategies for increasing your wealth and managing your finances as you pursue your purpose and provide for yourself and your loved ones. Many of these are commonsense methods, but we have to make a specific decision to implement them. As we have seen, it's too easy to live by default rather than by design. You might be surprised at some of the simple things you can do that will make a significant difference to you financially and enable you to build wealth.

STRATEGIES FOR GAINING WEALTH AND MANAGING MONEY

As you review these strategies, note that several of these practices should be implemented sequentially, while others can be applied simultaneously.

LIST YOUR FINANCIAL PRIORITIES AND CREATE A BUDGET

To begin with, list your financial priorities, remembering that some of those priorities might not be immediate needs bur rather long-range goals. Think about the biggest expense you'll ever have in life. Is it your mortgage or your children's education? No. It's your retirement savings. Yet so few people prepare for retirement or other significant life costs. For example, it grieves me when I see people going through the funeral of a loved one, and the family barely has enough money to pay for even simple burial expenses. There are circumstances in which people unavoidably fall into financial straits; however, if we plan ahead to meet our monetary priorities and needs, we can greatly reduce the likelihood of finding ourselves in such a scenario.

After you have determined your financial priorities, establish a monthly budget for working toward long-term goals as you meet everyday needs. A budget is really a means of reinforcing your goals by setting parameters for you to spend and invest your money wisely. As you plan your budget, keep in mind that it's not enough just to live *within* your means; you need to live *beneath* your means in order to begin to build a surplus. We will cover this point more fully in the next section.

A BUDGET IS A MEANS OF REINFORCING YOUR
GOALS BY SETTING PARAMETERS FOR SPENDING
AND INVESTING YOUR MONEY WISELY.

LIVE BENEATH YOUR MEANS

One of the fastest ways to make money is to cut expenses. Use your creativity to start eliminating costs. There are many articles and books that give tips for reducing spending. You can also glean ideas from friends, relatives, and coworkers who are thrifty. Many people enjoy sharing stories of how they save money, so learn all you can.

Develop a spending plan for yourself in keeping with your budget so you know ahead of time what you can purchase and what you can't. Then exercise restraint. Some people use "retail therapy" to treat their emotional issues. Others feel they have a right to make a purchase because something is on sale, they received a coupon, it's their birthday, or other reasons. But no one can afford to buy frivolously—especially if they're already in debt.

One good principle is not to buy something unless you can get a good deal on it. As much as you can, plan ahead for what you will need, and purchase items when they are on sale or when the cost is reduced because they are out of season. Try to avoid shopping for something when you're desperate for it because you usually end up paying the highest price. You know how it's not wise to go grocery shopping when you're hungry, because either you buy too much or you buy the wrong kinds of things, like junk food? It's a similar principle. If you shop for high-cost items when you need them in a hurry, you will probably end up going by your feelings alone rather than thinking things through carefully and making the best choices.

MAKE THE MOST OF WHAT YOU HAVE

Additionally, there are ways you can conserve the resources you already have and make the most of what you purchase. We often casually toss away what we might be able to reuse, and we don't always get the most for our money. One time, my brother and I were visiting one of our relatives in Chicago, and we were riding together in her car when she stopped to get gas. My brother pumped the gas for her, and he was about to put the nozzle back when she jumped out of the car, saying, "No, no, what are you doing?" She took the nozzle and shook it several times into the gas tank opening to get every drop of gasoline! It may not have amounted to much, but she didn't waste any of the gas, either.

Making the most of what we have is a good principle whether we use it on a small scale or a large scale. I have a friend who is worth six hundred million dollars. He has a thirty-two-million-dollar private jet, and he invited me to come with him on a trip to California. Before we left Atlanta, we flew from one airport in the city to another in order to fill up on gas. The total cost of the fuel for the trip was fifteen thousand dollars. I asked him, "Why didn't you just fill up at the first airport?" He told me that the gas at the second airport was $1.10 cheaper per gallon, and that he had saved fifteen hundred dollars, saying, "I don't mind spending money, but I hate wasting money." He went out of his way to save fifteen hundred dollars, even though he is worth six hundred million. But that is the mind-set that has enabled him to build wealth.

So think about your habits in relation to how you use material goods, food, and other items, and consider ways in which you might be wasting something you will have to go out and buy again unnecessarily or sooner than needed. And look for both large and small ways to conserve in order to save money in the long run.

SYSTEMATICALLY GET OUT OF DEBT

The book of Proverbs says, "The rich rule over the poor, and the borrower is servant to the lender."[29] If you borrow, you essentially become a servant to whomever the lender is, whether it is a bank, a business, a family member, or a friend. When you borrow from someone, especially a financial institution, they put conditions on the loan—what the interest rate will be, when the loan must be paid in full, and so forth—and you have obligated yourself to pay them back when you don't know what your financial future will be. All of this makes you a servant to the lender because you have no control over those conditions.

Some institutions draw people in with loan offers that advertise 0 percent financing for a certain period of time, such as the first six months. However, there's no such a thing as a charity loan. Trust me—they're probably going to get their money on the back end of the loan if not the front end, so read the fine print.

We should never borrow money to pay for things like clothing and vacations because those are depreciating assets and are therefore bad debt. There are certain things for which the value of what you purchase through a loan will generally appreciate, such as a home mortgage, so it is considered "good debt." But don't borrow more than you're going to have the ability to repay. Anything like credit card or department store charges will just cause you to go deeper in the hole unless you can pay off the balance in full

---

29. Proverbs 22:7.

without straining yourself when the bill comes due. Finance fees will eat up your money. If you are in debt more than 10 percent of your gross annual salary, that's a huge red flag to your finances.

As you begin to live beneath your means, however, you can start to pay off any debts you have. Make it a priority to pay off all of your debt as soon as possible because of the interest you are paying on it. You can even pay off a loan for a car or a home earlier than originally planned. If you add just a little extra to your payment each time, you can save a lot of money in interest charges. After you pay off one bill, use the amount you had been applying toward that bill to pay off another bill, and so forth. For the sake of integrity, pay back all of your debt, even if it takes you a while.

Another aspect of debt is that it isn't advisable to cosign or become a guarantor for a loan for someone who is irresponsible with their money or who has other character issues; they are a very high risk, and you may end up with bad credit. You can control your own actions, but you can't control somebody else's actions. Some people don't fully understand what it means to cosign. If you cosign for somebody who wants to buy a car, for example, and they fall behind on the payments, you become responsible for that debt. If you're not willing to take that risk, don't cosign.

WHEN YOUR OUTPUT EXCEEDS YOUR INCOME,
THEN YOUR UPKEEP BECOMES YOUR DOWNFALL.

ACCUMULATE SAVINGS

After you get out of debt, you can start saving and investing. Make a plan for generating savings. For example, if you put away even twenty dollars a week, perhaps forgoing a couple of fast-food lunches or giving up something else that is not essential, you can save over a thousand dollars in a year.

You might not be able to start off doing this right away, but work on getting to a place where you can save at least ten percent of your income. It's often good to create separate accounts for short-term savings and long-term savings so you won't dip into the money you are saving for long-range priorities. For goals that will be met in five years or less, you can set aside funds in a separate savings account, in a money market account, or in a Certificate of Deposit (CD). Research to see what option is best for you, making adjustments, as needed, as market conditions change or you find a better interest rate at a different bank or other financial institution.

Your savings plan should include putting money aside for retirement. You might use a 401k plan, a traditional Individual Retirement Account (IRA), a Roth IRA, or another plan. You will need to discipline yourself to do this. Many people arrange to have a certain amount of money deposited automatically from their paycheck into their retirement plan or savings account so they're not tempted to use it for other things.

DO NOT SAVE WHAT IS LEFT AFTER SPENDING BUT SPEND WHAT IS LEFT AFTER SAVING.

CREATE ADDITIONAL INCOME STREAMS

Most people depend on only a single income stream, such as a job or business. It is wise to create a second, third, and even fourth source of income for yourself, whether through earnings or investments, because anything could happen to any one of those streams. In our world today, we're dealing with rapid change on every hand—sociological change, technological change, economic change, environmental change, and political change. Some once-dependable careers are quickly heading toward obsolescence. Occupations people were trained to do twenty or thirty years ago are drying up. In an uncertain economy, you might get laid off from your job. Or your business might go under unexpectedly. Or your life circumstances might change. For example, you might want to stop working full-time for a period in order to care for an elderly or ill family member. Situations such as these create a need to generate income in a new or different way than you have been. We should always have a skill in reserve that we can rely on if necessary. As I expressed earlier, as we follow the wisdom journey, we need to be flexible in the way we pursue our overall purpose, and in how it may manifest in various seasons and expressions.

Companies that do well often diversify in order to generate additional income and to stay relevant in the marketplace. Sometimes they purchase another company that is not specifically related to the main business that initially made them successful. The acquisition allows them to have additional funds to invest into the primary business or to use as a buffer for it. We can employ the same principle in our lives, generating secondary income to supplement our chief income stream as we pursue our calling or vision.

How can we expand our earnings sources? Our additional income streams, like our primary stream, will be related to our unique gifting and skills. These may or may not directly pertain to our primary gift. While we should focus on our dominant gift, we can often use secondary gifts to generate subsidiary income streams. Many people don't realize the money-making creativity and abilities within them.

As you consider developing additional streams, keep in mind that whenever we generate income, we are paid for *what we know* or *what we can do*—or both. We trade our knowledge and creativity and ideas and skills and productivity for compensation. Having more goods or services available to trade gives us more potential access to income. So find out what other people want in relation to what you are gifted in. Your second (or subsequent) stream might be any of the following—consulting for corporations, designing and maintaining web sites, writing magazine articles, giving motivational talks, doing people's taxes, tutoring children in a particular subject, teaching music lessons, cutting and styling hair, designing greeting cards, selling gourmet cookies, offering cooking lessons, washing cars, doing landscaping—or a multitude of other possibilities. Develop a trade or business that matters to people because it fills a need in their life or aids in the growth or security of their company. Sometimes a secondary stream becomes so successful that it outperforms a primary stream.

No one is going to exchange their wealth for your talent or creativity if you don't provide an avenue for it to be traded. There were two young guys in their twenties who saw a need and created a company called Dropbox. Steve Jobs immediately saw its potential and set up a meeting with them. He offered to buy their company for a nine-figure price—but they turned him down. They knew the tremendous value of their idea, and they understood they had a strong bargaining chip to be able to trade in the marketplace. Now their company is worth billions. Whatever you choose to do, on a large or small scale, develop something of value, and know the value of what you have.

HAVING MORE GOODS OR SERVICES AVAILABLE TO TRADE GIVES US MORE POTENTIAL ACCESS TO INCOME.

OWN YOUR OWN HOME

I believe that homeownership is the foundation for all other wealth-building, and that it usually makes financial sense to buy your own home rather than renting. It's difficult to get ahead while you're renting because although you will receive some services from the rental property owners in exchange for your money, none of that money will come back to you the way it would if you owned your own home and decided to sell it. Many people don't realize that rent is often just as high as a mortgage—sometimes higher. If you become a homeowner, you can start building equity. You will need to factor in additional home maintenance and insurance expenses into your budget, but you will gain in the long run.

MAKE WISE INVESTMENTS

Note that you are not ready to invest until you get out of debt. It doesn't make sense to invest in something that will pay you even a 6 percent return if you're already paying out 23 percent on your credit-card debt. But if you have paid off your debt, investing wisely will enable you to multiply your investment instead of multiplying your debt.

BORROWING MONEY ROBS FROM YOUR FUTURE
TO ENHANCE YOUR PRESENT, BUT INVESTING
MONEY WITHDRAWS FROM YOUR PRESENT
TO ENHANCE YOUR FUTURE.

While *borrowing* money robs from your future to enhance your present, *investing* money withdraws a certain amount from your present to enhance your future. Additionally, savings only adds to us, while investing multiplies to us. And in the current economy, interest rates for savings accounts add very little to the principal. So consider investing some of the money that you have begun to save or that you are generating through a secondary income stream.

When you invest, it's best to diversify. Don't put all of your eggs into one basket. And avoid investing in anything you don't understand. A friend may tell you about a "great" investment opportunity, but you might not be able to learn enough about it to gauge whether it is likely to do well. Use caution and don't fall into any "get-rich-quick" schemes. Find a reputable broker and then research what is being offered so you can make the best choice.

Remember that the things that give the highest return involve the greatest risk. Generally, the younger you are, the more you can invest in higher-yield plans that have higher risk, but you will still want to diversify. If you put everything into one entity and that fails, you will lose everything you have invested. The older you get, the less risk you can afford to take, because you have less time to make up the difference if the market takes a downturn or a fund performs poorly. As people grow older, they usually switch to more conservative investments.

UTILIZE FREE MONEY

If you are employed by a company that matches its employees' 401k retirement fund contributions dollar for dollar, strongly consider utilizing that option. You build additional savings for retirement without it costing you anything. A 401k plan will allow you to defer taxes on the money until you retire and start drawing from it. There are advantages and disadvantages to plans that defer taxes, so determine which plan is right for you. There may also be additional benefits and savings that your company offers or that you can obtain through other businesses or organizations with which you are associated. Make use of all the free money available to you.

INSURE YOURSELF

Homeowner or rental insurance, life insurance, automobile insurance, and other forms of insurance protect your assets. While you can even borrow against some insurance policies, never use your life insurance policies as an investment. Buy life insurance to provide death benefits and to give your survivors some money to live on until your estate is settled.

ESTABLISH AN EMERGENCY FUND

It's not a matter of *if* storms (either literal or figurative) will come into our lives, but *when*. What if you were suddenly faced with exorbitant medical bills or had to take long-term medical leave? What if you were out of a job for a year? Suppose you found yourself dealing with an expensive lawsuit through no fault of your own? What if the business deal you thought was a wonderful opportunity ended up being a business nightmare, so that you lost money instead of making it? What if your car needed extensive repairs at the same time a major appliance needed to be replaced? What if your house was flooded after a hurricane? Do you have a plan to provide funds for such possibilities?

These kinds of things happen at the most inopportune times, don't they? For example, appliances never break down when your bank account is running over with money! As I wrote in the chapter "Wisdom Plans Ahead," in discussing such things, I'm not trying to be negative, just practical; we need to expect problems and make provision ahead of time for emergencies. Building an emergency fund will lessen the temptation or the need for you to dip into your long-term savings during those times; it will give you a financial cushion to be ready for the unexpected and the inevitable.

GIVE CHARITABLY

I believe that giving charitably to benevolent causes, such as a humanitarian organization or one's local church, will come back to us at some point in a form of blessing—financial or otherwise. What we give to others might leave our hand but it won't leave our life. Jesus taught, "Give, and it will be given to you. A good measure, pressed down, shaken together and running over, will be poured into your lap. For with the measure you use, it will be measured to you."[30] And Proverbs says, "Honor the LORD with your possessions, and with the firstfruits of all your increase; so your barns will be filled with plenty, and your vats will overflow with new wine.[31]

Apart from any material returns that may come back to us from helping others, the act of giving provides us with well-being in other ways. For example, a few years ago, I heard about some research that caught my attention because it indicated you can buy happiness—as long as you don't spend the money on yourself. The researchers conducted an experiment in which people were randomly given either five dollars or twenty dollars. Some were told to spend the money on themselves, while others were told to give it away—all before five o'clock the same afternoon. What happened at the end of the day? The researchers reported:

> Individuals who spent money on others—who engaged in what
> we call "prosocial spending"—were measurably happier than those
> who spent money on themselves—even though there were no dif-
> ferences between the two groups at the beginning of the day....

30. Luke 6:38 (NIV).
31. Proverbs 3:9–10.

How people spent the money mattered much more than how much of it they got.[32]

When people gave to others, whether it was just five dollars or twenty dollars, it made them feel happier. This was the case even though the giving was an "assignment." This corroborates the biblical principle that "it is more blessed to give than to receive."[33] We often imagine that buying and having things will make us happier; but ultimately, giving to others will not only benefit the ones who receive but will also lift us up, bringing us more joy and satisfaction in life.

Let me add in conclusion that we should always exercise good judgment when we give, rather than donate indiscriminately, because unfortunately there are certain people out there who seek to manipulate generous people with scams in order to take their money. There are also organizations that waste charitable donations through mismanagement. Groups like Charity Navigator can help you identify the best charities. We don't have to allow some people's bad motivations or poor administration to keep us from reaching out in compassion to those who are in need, and from using our surplus to make a better future for others.

"THE ONLY WEALTH WHICH YOU WILL KEEP FOREVER
IS THE WEALTH YOU HAVE GIVEN AWAY."
—MARCUS AURELIUS

REVIEW YOUR FINANCIAL HABITS MONTHLY

Revisit your spending and savings plans as well as your overall financial goals monthly to make sure you're on track. If you don't continually evaluate your financial habits and plans, you can't improve them, and you won't

32. Elizabeth W. Dunn and Michael I. Norton, "How to Make Giving Feel Good," June 18, 2013, https://greatergood.berkeley.edu/article/item/how_to_make_giving_feel_good.
33. Acts 20:35.

really know in which direction you are moving fiscally or be able to gauge your progress.

HELPFUL TIPS AND REMINDERS

Here are some helpful tips and reminders as you put the above strategies into practice:

+ *Remember to pay yourself.* It's easy to get caught up in paying bills and other expenses so that we pay everybody else but forget to pay ourselves to build our future. Make saving and investing a habit.

+ *Begin early—the earlier the better.* That means now. If you are young, don't wait to begin saving. If you are older and should have begun to save years ago but have neglected to do so, the next best time is right now.

+ *Start small.* Begin with what you have, and do as much as you can with what you have, even if it's only a small amount.

+ *Be consistent.* Once you start to save and invest, keep consistent with it because it's easy to lose sight of your goals and get off track. Again, you might arrange to have money direct-deposited from your paycheck into your savings or investment account to maintain your financial growth. Your money will eventually add up.

+ *Educate yourself.* To make the best fiscal choices, learn more about budgeting, financial planning, and investing through reputable books, Internet sites, seminars, and conferences, as well as the trusted knowledge and experience of family members, friends, and acquaintances.

+ *Establish an income stream before expanding it.* As you create additional income streams, don't expand an endeavor that is not yet producing a profit, because it will drain your resources. For example, if the initial location of your business is not yet solvent, it isn't wise to open up a second location. You need to expect a learning curve as you gain proficiency from your experience, grow from your mistakes, and discover how to make the endeavor successful. Once you start seeing a profit and have more than enough funds to maintain and grow the first business, you can consider expanding.

+ *Always exercise integrity.* Proverbs says, "Wealth gained by dishonesty will be diminished, but he who gathers by labor will increase."[34] Always use integrity in your financial dealings and as you trade your goods or services. Nobody will stay in business for long if they are fraudulent with customers, if they don't honor their word, and if they don't maintain good customer service. They will create negative PR, and the word will spread. Business is about building relationships with customers and developing repeat business as well as new patrons. Besides being the right thing to do, it pays to treat people with integrity and respect.

+ *Recognize that building wealth takes careful planning, hard work, and perseverance.* Wealth-building is never as easy as some people make it look. We see their results, but we don't see the work behind the scenes. Working hard and working smart as you follow wisdom principles will lead to financial gain.

BENEFITS OF A WISDOM-DRIVEN LIFE

+ Identifying our financial priorities and planning ahead enables us to meet our monetary needs and goals.

+ Establishing a monthly budget allows us to work toward long-term priorities as we meet everyday needs; it also reinforces our goals by setting parameters by which we can spend and invest our money wisely.

+ We can begin to build surplus wealth by spending less than we earn, making the most of what we have, systematically getting out of debt, accumulating savings, creating additional income streams, owning our own home, making wise investments, utilizing free money, establishing an emergency fund, giving charitably, and monthly reviewing our financial habits, plans, and goals.

+ Working hard and working smart as you follow wisdom principles will lead to financial gain.

---

34. Proverbs 13:11.

APPLYING WISDOM

1. How many of the financial strategies in this chapter are you currently following?

2. In what areas might you improve or expand?

3. In what ways could you use your dominant gift or secondary gifts to generate additional income streams?

4. Make a plan to implement at least one new financial strategy this month—and act on it.

PART 3
WISDOM CLEARS AWAY THE OBSTACLES

11

WISDOM POSTPONES PROCRASTINATION

"The only difference between success and failure is
the ability to take action."
—Alexander Graham Bell

Throughout this book, we've been looking at strategic wisdom principles for success. There are many things we can do that will enable us to better follow our life purpose and grow personally and professionally. Yet I often see people who want to accomplish their dreams and goals, who understand the principles—but hold back. They hesitate from taking that first step. Or they make a good start and then get stalled in the process because they don't seem to be able to take the next step. They end up procrastinating and thus losing much time in which they could have been pursing and attaining important life goals. As Benjamin Franklin sagely said, "You may delay, but time will not."

All of us have procrastinated about something. It might be an endeavor as significant as getting started on the vision for our life or a task as small as a simple daily chore. For various reasons, we delay, we stall, or we wait around for something to happen rather than take action.

Why do we sometimes procrastinate about things we *want* to do, not only the things we *don't* want to do? And what should we do when we just can't seem to begin or take the next step? The wisdom-driven life directs us to discover and address the causes of our procrastination, freeing us to move ahead so we can successfully accomplish both what we want to do and what we need to do. This chapter will reinforce some the principles we've previously covered while showing how to enter into them more fully.

"YOU MAY DELAY, BUT TIME WILL NOT."
—BENJAMIN FRANKLIN

REASONS WE PROCRASTINATE

The following are reasons time management experts and others have given for why people procrastinate.

FEAR AND WORRY

Most people have a tendency to put off what they fear doing. I can't tell you how often people's fears keep them from acting on something even when they have a deep desire to do it. We might fear being criticized or laughed at, or we might fear we aren't up to the task. We might be afraid of the unknown, or we might lack the courage to embark on a new course in life. Or we might worry about failing.

Worry is a particularly destructive form of fear because it gnaws at us and can paralyze us from making any progress. It makes it difficult for us to think clearly because we are continually focused on the idea that something negative will happen. Seth Godin wrote, "Anxiety is nothing...but repeatedly re-experiencing failure in advance."[35]

---

35. See sethgodin.typepad.com/seths_blog/2010/03/anxiety-is-nothing-but-repeatedly-experiencing-failure-in-advance.html.

FEELING OVERCOMMITTED OR OVERWHELMED

Another reason for procrastination is a feeling of being overcommitted. Have you ever committed yourself to something and then kicked yourself afterward because you really didn't have the time to do it? Having too much to do on many different levels in our life can cause us to be emotionally or mentally stymied, because all the various responsibilities seem to be pulling at us at the same time. We don't know which task to begin first or how we can possibly get everything done. We might wait until the last minute to take care of the most urgent need of the moment, causing ourselves stress and lack of sleep, and perhaps straining our relationships.

In a related way, we might procrastinate when faced with a particular job or assignment that seems too big for us to accomplish. Instead of tackling it, we may work on anything *but* that, including a number of smaller and less important tasks, leaving the big task undone. Or we may feel so weighed down that we don't work on anything at all. Many people wait until their feelings of being overwhelmed pass before they get back into motion and resume working on something. But by then, there is often some damage done or some consequence to face—a missed window of opportunity because a business proposal was never written, an angry client who expected a job to be completed, penalties from the IRS because of unpaid taxes, and so on.

INDECISIVENESS

Another reason people procrastinate is that they are stuck in indecision about which course to take or which choice to make. Once I went to a restaurant whose menu had *five hundred* items on it. I'd never been there before, so I didn't know what entrées were particularly good; I didn't have a lot information to go on in making a final choice. Our waitress immediately came over to the table, took our drink orders, and said, "Are you ready to order?" I said, "It's going to be a minute! Give me some time." I just couldn't decide what I wanted to eat. Life can feel like that at times. We are faced with either too many options or two or three good choices that make it difficult to make a specific decision, especially because we want to make the best decision. We don't know how to make a final choice, so we decide not to decide, even though a choice really needs to be made.

LACK OF A DEADLINE

The lack of a specific deadline can often cause us to put off working on a project. If no one is expecting something from us at a particular time, we might begin to think it's not really important when it gets done, if at all. Or we develop the false perspective that we have all the time in the world to complete it. This mind-set is especially problematic for people who work for themselves or who are independently working on personal development goals where the motivation has to come totally from within, not from an outside source.

UNCLEAR INSTRUCTIONS OR GOALS

Most of us have had the experience of traveling on vacation or going on a business trip where we've stayed at a hotel or at the home of a friend who lives in the area. We wake up in the night feeling thirsty and want to get a glass of water, but the room is dark and we're in an unfamiliar environment. In those cases, we don't just get up and stride to the bathroom or kitchen to get the drink of water because we're not fully oriented to where the furniture in the room is or how the house is arranged, and we don't want to bump into something. We may decide to just wait until morning. If we do get up, we often have to move slowly across the room until we can find a light switch or open a door to let some light in. Similarly, if our instructions about a particular task are confusing or our goals for an endeavor are unclear, we will feel in the dark about things, and we may set aside an assignment to work on something else we understand better. Or if we do work on it, we merely inch along, making little progress until we can get some clarity on it.

RESENTMENT

When we resent doing a task, we often delay getting started on it. Sometimes, in the workplace, when people receive an assignment they consider difficult or unreasonable, even unnecessary, they may think, *They're not paying me enough to be doing that!* Because they resent doing what they've been asked to do, the task gets pushed very low on their priority list, and they may put it off indefinitely.

Sometimes it may not be the task itself that they resent, but the person who asked them to do it. They might have had prior disagreements or clashes in temperament with the person; or they might feel the person has treated them badly or undermined them. Even though they know they should be working on the assignment, they reject it because they want to be in control of the situation; they feel that if they do what the person is telling them to do, it's a form of surrender, and they don't want to feel vulnerable or be hurt again. Whatever the reason for the resentment, the job doesn't get done.

DISTRACTIONS

Interruptions are not always distractions; sometimes, they are necessary or unavoidable in the course of our life and work. But true distractions tempt us to do something that is more enjoyable or interesting than the task at hand. We might be at our desk at work on a Monday morning when a coworker stops by to deliver something, and the visit turns into an hour-long discussion about the ball game on Sunday and what the home team's chances are this year. Or we're researching something for our business on the Internet when we see a side story about a totally unrelated topic, but we read it anyway just because it's more fun than what we're working on. Distractions can eat up much of our time, causing us to delay making progress on important goals and projects.

FATIGUE

Sometimes, we find ourselves putting off tasks or not making much progress on them simply because we are physically fatigued, making it difficult to concentrate well and work efficiently.

FEELING DOWN OR DEPRESSED

Feeling down is another common reason for procrastination. We become unmotivated to do anything because we are focused on thoughts that make us sad or discouraged. Moreover, true medical depression can cause people to lose interest in life, in their goals, and even in doing simple tasks.

PERFECTIONISM

People who have a tendency toward perfectionism may avoid starting on a task or making much headway on a project because they feel they won't be able to do it as well as they could or should due to time constraints, not enough preparation or research, or an environment that is not conducive. This keeps them from accomplishing various goals and responsibilities they are likely capable of completing well.

UNPLEASANT OR BORING TASKS

The simple reason that a task is unpleasant or boring often causes us to delay doing it. As we discussed previously, with every dream or vision, there are some tasks that need to be done even though they are not inspiring and may not use our primary gifting. When a job is messy, tedious, or thankless, there is a tremendous temptation to leave it for another time, even if doing so will slow us down in other ways.

WITH EVERY DREAM OR VISION,
THERE ARE SOME TASKS THAT NEED TO BE DONE
EVEN THOUGH THEY ARE NOT INSPIRING AND MAY
NOT USE OUR PRIMARY GIFTING.

THE DESIRE FOR ATTENTION

We might put off doing something if we don't think we will receive much recognition for it, and it doesn't advance our own agenda. We make it a low priority after more visible tasks that highlight our strengths and show others what we can do.

LAZINESS/APATHY

Let's admit it—sometimes we're just lazy and don't feel like doing something. Other times, we might feel no connection with a particular task or with the person who assigned us the job, so we become apathetic about it, and it remains undone. Achieving our goals and completing necessary tasks takes motivation, discipline, and effort.

PRACTICAL STRATEGIES FOR OVERCOMING PROCRASTINATION

Here are some practical strategies to help you move forward and make progress on your goals or assignments when you find yourself putting them off. These strategies can be applied to any area of life in which we are experiencing the symptoms of procrastination.

IDENTIFY THE UNDERLYING CAUSE(S)

First, you need to identify what specifically is contributing to your procrastination so you can know the best solutions to apply. Review the above reasons and determine which ones are influencing you to avoid doing what you want to do and need to do right now. For example, if fear or worry is the issue, what exactly are you anxious or worried about? Pinpoint the specific fear and acknowledge how it is affecting you. Then use the applicable solutions in the strategies that follow to move past those initial fears and get started.

SCHEDULE IT

If you tend to procrastinate about doing things for which there is no built-in time limit, remember that a goal is a dream with a deadline. Make a point to schedule what you want to do, setting up the time, the place, the space, and all the tools or resources you'll need to work effectively. Remember that you don't merely need to prioritize your schedule; you need to schedule your priorities—the things that are truly close to your heart. Otherwise, they won't get done.

We should never take time for granted. The psalmist wrote, "Teach us to number our days, that we may gain a heart of wisdom."[36] Act like you're not going to live forever (you aren't) so that you will begin to maximize your time now. In the chapter "Wisdom Creates Winning Habits, Part 2: Positive Practices for Success," we talked about "SMART" goals: the goals we establish for ourselves must be achievable, measurable, attainable,

36. Psalm 90:12.

realistic, and time-sensitive. So be sure to establish goals and then develop a schedule for completing them. This will help you to set deadlines and be accountable to yourself for working toward those goals.

NEVER TAKE TIME FOR GRANTED.

LEARN TO SAY "NO"

As we have seen, successful people have learned to say no to less important matters so they can say yes to activities and endeavors that align with their priorities. It often takes practice—and courage—to decline doing something optional or voluntary that someone asks you to do, especially when the person who is asking is a family member or friend. But learning to say no brings us freedom, helping us to avoid procrastination from overcommitment.

JUST GET STARTED!

Sometimes, when you find yourself putting off a task, the key is to just get started on it *somewhere*. If you feel overwhelmed by a major task, begin to work on one aspect of it, no matter how small. Often, you will quickly become involved in what you are doing, ideas will start to flow, and you will know how to continue and complete the job. And consider the advice of Dale Carnegie, who said, "Do the hard jobs first. The easy jobs will take care of themselves."

BREAK DOWN YOUR TASKS INTO MANAGEABLE PARTS

Additionally, when you're feeling overwhelmed by a large job, remember to break down your tasks into simpler, more manageable portions and work on them little by little. Think about it: do you manage your entire year at one time? Nobody does. We have to break yearly goals down into quarterly goals, quarterly goals into monthly goals, monthly goals into weekly goals, and weekly goals into daily goals. Sometimes daily goals have to be broken down into hourly goals.

Usually, it's not beneficial enough to work on something just once a week, although it may vary with the goal. If you have plans and aspirations for your life but make no place for them in your daily agenda, they will probably never happen. Try eating once a week. Try exercising once a week. Nobody will ever tell you that eating or exercising once a week is sufficient. As we have seen, success is found in our daily routines.

DELEGATE

You don't always have to do everything yourself. When you feel inundated and find yourself setting aside important tasks, learn to delegate certain jobs to others, taking some responsibilities off your plate. Please note that there's a huge difference between delegating and "dumping." If you give a job to somebody you know is irresponsible or not a good fit for the job, you didn't delegate but merely off-loaded the task because it will probably still be sitting there later. Dumping is thus the equivalent of continued procrastination. Instead, delegate tasks to responsible people whom you trust are competent to take care of them.

MAKE A DECISION

If you have a decision you must make, don't keep hanging between choices, oscillating back and forth and procrastinating. Choice, not chance, determines our destiny. Every choice is a decision to take responsibility, because with every choice there is a corresponding result or consequence. When you choose, you are saying, "I am willing to take the responsibility for this decision." That's why I don't make decisions for other people. I will help them with information that will equip them to make an informed decision, but they need to take that responsibility for themselves.

If you wait until you see the way ahead with perfect clarity, you will never decide. And if you wait until you have no more questions, you have probably waited too long. Indecision is a mark that you don't trust your judgment; you are not confident in your ability to make decisions. Martin Luther King Jr. said, "You don't have to see the whole staircase, just take the first step." As long as you can see the first step, you can take some action.

Choose to decide and take responsibility—even if it turns out to be a bad decision, at least you can learn something from it. You will learn not to do that again! Get all the input you can in order to make the most informed decision possible. Then don't be afraid to make a decision. Usually, once we decide, courage and energy are released in us. As the saying goes, "Success is not for the chosen few, but it's for the few who choose." Those who refuse to make a decision to choose will be surpassed by someone else who does have the courage to make that decision.

CHOICE, NOT CHANCE, DETERMINES OUR DESTINY.

STREAMLINE TASKS WHERE POSSIBLE

Streamlining tasks and becoming more efficient in them can also help us move past procrastination. Are you incorporating unnecessary steps into a project or task that causes it to take longer and feel more cumbersome, making you more inclined to put it off—or to put off other projects while you work on it? Would learning to be more efficient relieve you of some of the burden you're feeling? Take a little time to consider the process of what you are doing and how you might make changes to improve that process, reducing your load.

ELIMINATE DISTRACTIONS

When real distractions are keeping you from doing what you need to do, make a plan to remove them. For example, if your smart phone, iPad, or another electronic device tempts you away from working on a project, put it in another room or turn it off for a time. Work in a room where there is no television or Internet access. If you need to use the Internet for research, focus only on that research rather than checking your e-mail or clicking on news headlines or unrelated articles. If you see an online article that looks beneficial to you but is not connected to your immediate project, quickly save the URL, or web address, and go back to it later. If people are distracting you unnecessarily, be courteous but firm and clear about your need to focus on something without being interrupted. Closely guard and preserve your time.

GET CLARITY

Goals are like magnets—the clearer your goal, the more it pulls you toward it. Remember the scenario of being away from home and needing to get up at night in an unfamiliar environment, searching in the dark for a light switch? As soon as we find the switch and flip it on, we suddenly have clarity of vision, and we can move swiftly and confidently. Likewise, having clarity of vision for a goal or project will accelerate us in completing it.

If you are given an assignment at work that you don't fully understand, rather than put off the task, ask your supervisor or a coworker to explain it further. The confusion might be cleared up in five minutes. Or, if you are working toward your vision and come to a point where you don't know how to proceed, call or e-mail someone in the same field with whom you have established a professional relationship and ask what they think the next step should be. Read helpful books and look up relevant articles on the Internet. Don't be afraid to ask questions and to research answers when you feel uncertain. If you don't inquire, you can't learn—and you can't make progress.

GOALS ARE LIKE MAGNETS—THE CLEARER YOUR GOAL, THE MORE IT PULLS YOU TOWARD IT.

REFOCUS YOUR MOTIVATION

It's remarkable what a difference a little attitude adjustment can make in the midst of procrastination! For example, suppose you harbor resentment toward someone who gave you a task to do, so you delay the job. Once you acknowledge your motivation for postponing working on the project, you can refocus your perspective and change your actions. Don't allow those ill feelings to interfere with getting an important and necessary task completed. Release your resentment and do the job anyway for yourself and for the group, company, or organization as a whole. Seek to carry out your tasks with excellence regardless of who is delegating them. It will benefit you in the long run, and you will also feel much better about your performance.

GIVE YOURSELF A CHANGE OF PACE

When you get bogged down in a task, it can sometimes be helpful to take a short break for a change of pace—take a walk down the corridors of your workplace or stroll outside, get something to drink, make a quick call to a family member—something that will refresh your mind and spirit. You might even do a smaller job that needs to be done just to get your juices going (although don't allow yourself to get sidetracked with a lot of smaller jobs, which would merely extend your procrastination!).

Mark Twain joked, "Never put off till tomorrow what may be done day after tomorrow just as well." Putting off tasks is not normally advisable, and we have to be careful about this, but if a task can *truly* be done later and you're having trouble starting it, it might be beneficial to move on to something else for the time being so that you do *something* rather than *nothing*, making sure to reschedule the other task to be completed soon.

ALLOW YOURSELF NEEDED REST

If genuine fatigue is making it hard for you to start on a task or to concentrate on a project, you need to recognize your need for rest. As far are you are able at the time, get a respite before resuming your task, and make sure you get enough sleep at night. It's amazing how refreshed and ready for action we can feel after a short nap or a good night's sleep!

KEEP POSITIVE

Always try to keep positive about your goals and tasks. We can all become disappointed and discouraged at times. We may feel down, but we don't have to let our discouragement cause us to wallow in a pit of unhappiness and dejection so that we neglect our responsibilities. If we are feeling down, we need to change the focus of our thoughts to what is positive, and begin to take action again. (I will talk more about developing a positive mind-set in a later chapter.) When we experience mental or emotional fatigue, a little rest may also help, with this caution: we need to avoid allowing a legitimate need to rest at times to develop into a habit of sleeping to escape bad feelings or unpleasant responsibilities. And those who are experiencing true clinical depression need to seek professional counseling and/or medical assistance.

SET REMINDERS FOR YOURSELF

Set periodic reminders for yourself about projects and tasks, and the dates when they need to be completed. That way, if you do put off a task, you will be prompted that you need to get back to it in order to finish it on schedule. Use all the tools that are available to you when setting reminders—your smart phone, your computer, even old-fashioned paper and pen. You might have another person remind you about something important you have to do, whether large or small. For example, if someone you know gets up every morning like clockwork, but you consistently procrastinate about getting out of bed, you can ask them to call you to make sure you're up at a certain time.

GET A MUTUAL ACCOUNTABILITY PARTNER

This particular strategy is an extension of what we talked about in "Wisdom Develops Key Relationships, Part 2" regarding cultivating a relationship with someone to whom we can be accountable in life. Find an accountability partner who is also working on accomplishing a specific goal or project, and arrange a certain time to check up on each other. Meet or talk by phone weekly, or at least monthly, to say, for example, "I'm trying to increase my sales by 20 percent. I'm currently at 7 percent. How are you doing with your goal of taking on three new clients per week?" Sometimes it's easier for us to let ourselves down than it is to let somebody else down who believes in us and our objectives and is excited to hear about our progress.

AIM FOR EXCELLENCE INSTEAD OF "PERFECTION"

If you tend to procrastinate on tasks because you don't believe you can do them to a high enough standard, try changing the way you think about them. Always aim for excellence, of course, but don't try to attain an elusive goal of making something "perfect." If you have trouble knowing when you've reached a suitable stopping point, confer with someone you trust, such as a colleague in your field, a coworker, or an accountability partner. Just relax and do the best you can, even if you're not working under optimum conditions or with all the resources you might have wanted. Don't allow perfectionism to keep you from enjoying your work and making your contribution to the world.

REMIND YOURSELF OF PAST SUCCESSES

We've seen how a fear of failure can keep us from starting on an important goal, or delay us from making a change for the better. If we are too cautious, we may end up living our fears instead of our dreams. What we consider a "secure" life might actually be mediocrity in disguise. One way to get past fear is to remind yourself of things in which you've been successful in the past. Allow what you've accomplished previously to motivate you to try new things and to build upon your successes.

TRUTH BRINGS THE CONVICTION
NECESSARY FOR CHANGE.

"IF NOT NOW, WHEN?"

Are you stuck in procrastination? How long will you wait to start what you have always wanted to do, what you feel called to do, what you need to do? As the saying goes, "If not now, when? If not you, who?" We change when we learn enough about our situation that we want to change. We change when we receive enough guidance and help that we are able to change. And we change when we hurt enough that we *have* to change— when the pain of remaining the same becomes greater than the pain of changing. Otherwise, we keep going as we always have. Truth brings the conviction necessary for change. That's why, when we find ourselves procrastinating, we must recognize the need to take action and acknowledge that there is a way to do it.

Picasso reportedly said, "Only put off until tomorrow what you are willing to die having left undone." Don't postpone your vision or dream. Don't postpone important and necessary tasks. Postpone procrastination—indefinitely!

BENEFITS OF A WISDOM-DRIVEN LIFE

+   The wisdom-driven life directs us to discover and address the causes of our procrastination, freeing us to move ahead so we can successfully accomplish both what we want to do and what we need to do.

+   We can overcome procrastination by identifying the underlying cause, scheduling a goal or task, learning to say "no," just getting started, breaking down a task into manageable parts, delegating, making a decision to do something, streamlining tasks, eliminating distractions, getting clarity, refocusing our motivation, giving ourselves a change of pace, allowing ourselves needed rest, keeping positive, setting reminders, getting a mutual accountability partner, aiming for excellence instead of "perfection," and reminding ourselves of past successes.

+   Truth brings the conviction necessary for change.

APPLYING WISDOM

1. In what areas are you procrastinating about pursuing an important goal or doing a particular task?

2. What effect is your procrastination having on you—your peace of mind, your relationships, your progress in life?

3. Which strategy (or strategies) in this chapter best addresses your particular form of procrastination? How can you begin today to implement that strategy?

12

WISDOM GIVES LIFE BALANCE

"The key to keeping your balance is knowing when you've lost it."
—Anonymous

OFF BALANCE

While seeking to attain their goals and be successful, many people overlook a most important aspiration: to achieve true balance in one's life—spiritually, physically, and intellectually. Contributing to this common oversight is our tremendously busy lives. We give ourselves so totally to the task of raising a family, running a home, building a career, maintaining our relationships, trying to fulfill our volunteer commitments, and dealing with the various circumstances and difficulties of our lives that we often forget the need to nurture our spirit, body, and mind. We're so occupied just trying to keep up that we don't make ongoing provision for our own personal renewal and growth.

To make this provision, we need to learn to care for ourselves. There is nothing wrong with taking time to do good things for yourself. This is not selfishness but wisdom. Selfishness is depriving another person in order to benefit yourself alone. There are things we all need to do to maintain our health and strength, to keep our mind sharp, and to cultivate a peaceful spirit. In doing so, we will not only build ourselves up personally, but we will also make ourselves more fit to care for our loved ones and to energetically pursue our purpose.

A BALANCE OF INGREDIENTS

Anybody who is a good cook knows you need a balance of ingredients if you want to create a dish that is full of flavor. And experienced chefs understand that balance does not necessarily mean equal parts—it means having the right proportion of the various ingredients. Have you ever had lemonade that was too tart because it had a disproportionate amount of lemon juice in it, or that was too sweet because there was a disproportionate amount of sugar in it? The ingredients were not combined correctly for the most enjoyable taste. Or consider a balance beam scale, where you have a certain amount of weight on one side, and a certain amount on the other side. You might have ten of one substance on one side, and only seven of another substance on the other side, but the weight balances out.

FOCUSING ON BOTH PERSONAL RENEWAL
AND PERSONAL GROWTH WILL GIVE US
VITAL BALANCE IN LIFE.

Similarly, having the correct "ingredients" spiritually, physically, and mentally provides us with much-needed balance, leading to a life that is truly prosperous—in the fullest sense of the word. Maintaining balance does not usually mean devoting the same amount of time each day to spirit, body, and mind. Balance is a point between extremes, and our life is in constant flux, with the point continually shifting and moving. We may have to devote more time on a given day or week in one area or to address a particular issue to bring our life back into balance. For this reason, we need to be flexible and able to adjust to the various situations and phases of our life, while being on the lookout for symptoms indicating that an area of our life is out of proportion.

Achieving balance does not occur overnight. It takes trial and error and an increasing understanding of the various aspects of our life that need to be developed to attain a healthy equilibrium. Focusing on both *personal renewal* and *personal growth* will facilitate this vital balance.

BALANCE THROUGH PERSONAL RENEWAL

First, let's look at the foundation for personal renewal. The Creator apparently thought that human beings needed to be regularly renewed because He included a day of rest as one of the Ten Commandments.[37] He said, in effect, "Once a week, stop what you're doing, and take just one day as a divine Sabbath to honor Me and be refreshed." The word for "Sabbath," *Shabbat*, literally means "intermission," and it comes from a word than means "to repose" or "to desist from exertion."[38] The intent was for people to set aside, for a period of time, whatever they would normally be doing, for purposes of restoration.

Many people today think of the idea of "Sabbath" as the imposition of rules and prohibitions, but let's look at it as a wisdom principle. It was actually given as a gift. It was meant as a time for honoring the Creator, for spending time with family and friends, and for resting one's spirit, body, and mind. It was a time to cease from most of the daily routines in order to be restored to take them up again.

People of faith differ on how the Sabbath should specifically be observed, but the principle is that we need to set aside a block of time each week to experience the benefits of such an extended period of rest. I believe that when we do this, the result will reflect the "slingshot principle": if we will pull back one day a week, the other six days will be more effective. Many busy people don't understand this principle and instead cram in as much as they can every day of the week, for as many hours as they can put

---

37. See Exodus 20:8.
38. *Strong's Exhaustive Concordance of the Bible* (#H7676).

in. They think they are being more effective, but they may just be working harder and wearing themselves out, even putting their health in danger.

THE "SLINGSHOT PRINCIPLE": IF WE WILL PULL BACK ONE DAY A WEEK, THE OTHER SIX DAYS WILL BE MORE EFFECTIVE.

When we put our whole self into doing anything—working at the office, writing at the computer, doing physical labor at a work site, or maintaining a home—it flows from the deepest part of our being, necessitating times of renewal. If we don't allow for those times, we will lose part of ourselves in our busyness. Or when we have given our whole self to other people—nurturing children, caring for someone who is sick, dealing with a difficult relationship—we will need times of rejuvenation. So often, we try to give and give and give, and we don't always realize how weary and drained we have become. If we only give out and never take in, eventually, we're going to run dry. Some people resort to taking pills to keep going because they haven't built in time for personal restoration.

Do you usually have to yank energy from somewhere inside you just to get through the day? When was the last time you took a full day or a period of time when you didn't browse the Internet or send text messages or do all the other things you normally do during the rest of the week?

We read in the Psalms, "He leads me beside the still waters."[39] We need times when we are in the stillness, away from the churning of the world, so that we can regain our strength and perspective. Just as being near a tranquil lake or a quiet stream often makes us feel more peaceful, taking time for a tranquil "intermission" in our lives helps to restore our calm. We might not always be able to take off a full day to rest, but we should try to incorporate the equivalent into our week.

---

39. Psalm 23:2.

There's another benefit to such stillness. In the ancient world, people used clear, still water as a type of mirror to help them see what they really looked like. When we're pushing ourselves six days out of the week, we need to be able to stop and look into something that gives us a reflection of who we really are—not something man-made, but something that helps us to see from the perspective of our Creator so our soul can be restored.

In addition to the longer period of rest weekly, we should apply the basic principle of "intermission" daily at various points throughout our day. We require short periods when we can take a break from work and other responsibilities to give our minds rest, our bodies exercise, and our spirits refreshment.

BALANCE THROUGH PERSONAL GROWTH

Our second focus for creating balance in our lives is personal growth. A common practice many people fall into is to work *in* their environment but not *on* their environment to make enhancements and necessary improvements. For example, someone might work *in* their business much of the time but never work *on* their business, developing it and building it up. Someone might work *in* their home much of the time but never work *on* their home, adapting it to best facilitate their family's lifestyle and creating a haven from outside pressures. Someone might function *in* their marriage relationship all the time but never work *on* their relationship, making a point to nurture their bond with their spouse rather than falling into mere coexistence.

Similarly, with regard to our spirit, body, and mind, none of those aspects of our life is going to improve by simply working *in* it; we have to purposefully work *on* it. When we do, our life will become more satisfying, fruitful, and peaceful. As with other goals, we have to intentionally create time and space for personal growth. The following are some simple and practical ways you can achieve more balance in your life by nurturing your spirit, strengthening your body, and challenging your mind.

1. NURTURE YOUR SPIRIT

Perhaps you have never given much thought to nurturing your spirit. French philosopher Pierre Teilhard de Chardin wrote, "You are not a human being in search of a spiritual experience. You are a spiritual being immersed in a human experience." Our spirit is the essence of who we are as human beings, created in God's image. The more we nurture our spirit, the better life we will have and the greater peace we will gain: "To be spiritually minded is life and peace."[40] We nurture our spirit by connecting with God in prayer and worship, by reading Scripture and books on spiritual topics, by meeting with others for mutual spiritual growth and encouragement, as well as by giving to those in need with our time, talents, and money.

There's a story told about a rabbi who stops a prominent member of his congregation in the street and says to him, "Whenever I see you, you're always in a hurry. You're always rushing somewhere. Tell me, what are you running after all the time?" The man answers, "I'm running after success. I'm running after prosperity. I'm running after a good living."

The rabbi responds, "That's a good answer if you assume that all of those rewards are out ahead of you trying to elude you, and you have to run hard to catch up to them; but what if the rewards are behind you looking for you but can never find you because you're running away from them? What if God has all sorts of wonderful gifts that He wants to give you, but you've never home when He comes looking for you so He can't deliver them?"

That idea of needing to be "at home" when God comes to visit reminds me of something Catherine of Sienna wrote about. She advised a close friend to make two homes for herself—one actual home and another spiritual home that she would carry with her always.[41] To me, making a spiritual home involves nurturing our spirit through a personal relationship with God. We don't need to be inside a church or another religious place of worship to be connected to the Creator. We carry our spiritual home with us wherever we go if we have nurtured our spirit, enabling us to receive the gifts God has for us. For instance, if we become frustrated at work, we can take a short break to slip into an empty office or just sit at our desk and reach out to God to receive His peace and direction.

---

40. Romans 8:6.
41 Catherine of Siena, "Saint Catherine of Siena as Seen in Her Letters," https://books.google.com/books?id=LWNjf0Z4lyQC&pg=PA27&lpg=PA27& dq=catherine+of+siena+one+actual+home&source.

2. STRENGTHEN YOUR PHYSICAL BODY

The second aspect of personal development is to strengthen our physical body. Our body is the single most precious asset we have for functioning in life. Moreover, the state of our physical body can have a significant influence on our mind and emotions. Being careless about our health and allowing ourselves to become ill keeps us from being able to do all the things we need to do and want to do. Three major ways in which we can strengthen our body are by nourishing it, exercising it, and resting it.

OUR BODY IS THE SINGLE MOST PRECIOUS ASSET WE
HAVE FOR FUNCTIONING IN LIFE.

Nourishing the Body

Not everything that feeds us nourishes us. We should think about it in this way: generally, whatever we put into our body is either promoting health or encouraging sickness. If we consistently eat foods that are high in fat and sugar, we are putting ourselves at risk for illnesses like diabetes and heart disease. Some people imagine they can just say a blessing over their food, no matter what it consists of, and God will remove all of the bad things from it, without their needing to take responsibility to eat nutritiously. That is not wise living—it is presumption.

Here are some simple ways to nourish your body. As always, especially if this is an area of imbalance in your life, start with small, simple steps, and make gentle improvements as you go.

1. Review your typical daily meals. Again, before you can make improvements, you have to assess where you are, so review your typical daily meals and snacks. Determine what you are eating regularly. Then, for each food item, ask yourself, *Is this food promoting health or encouraging sickness?* That doesn't mean we can't enjoy ice cream or other treats at times, but a steady diet of such foods will not provide the nutritional balance we need.

2. Select one food that you would do well to eat less often. Begin with removing just one unhealthy food item from your diet. Think in terms of cutting down on fried foods, fatty foods, foods with excess salt, packaged foods that are highly processed, and foods with white sugar, white flour, or white rice.

3. Select one food that you would do well to eat more often. Think of fresh fruits and vegetables and whole grains. Even here, we need to use wisdom in our choices. A column published in *Scientific American* reported that "fruits and vegetables grown decades ago were much richer in vitamins and minerals than the varieties most of us get today. The main culprit in this disturbing nutritional trend is soil depletion." Reportedly, there was a significant decline in the nutritional value of fruits and vegetables grown during the last half of the twentieth century, with the trend continuing into the twenty-first century. That doesn't mean that our fruits and vegetables today have *no* nutritional value; even though they contain less nutritional value than previously, they are still a vital source of nourishment, and an important food group for us to consume. However, the best nutrient-rich fruits and vegetables today are organically grown ones.[42]

Exercising the Body

In our culture, it's difficult to provide our body with the physical activity it needs without making a specific plan for it. In earlier times, people's lifestyle was very different from ours. Their physical activity was integrated into their everyday lives, and it was much more intense; thus, they needed to eat more calories than we do in order to sustain their bodies and keep up their strength. Can you imagine having to go out and hunt your own food, or walking several miles to the nearest store to get groceries? Can you imagine cleaning your clothes in a big tub with a wash board or on the rocks of a riverbank, or using an old-fashioned, heavy iron that doesn't run on electricity but is heated on a stove? (I'm sure they really got a shoulder workout using that!) It wasn't very long ago that many families still did much more physical labor on a day-to-day basis than we do today. My father was one of eleven children, and somebody once asked him if they had

---

42. Roddy Scheer and Doug Moss, "EarthTalk," https://www.scientificamerican.com/article/soil-depletion-and-nutrition-loss/.

running water. He answered, "Yeah, we had running water; we'd run down to the well and get it!"

As you can imagine, with all of the physical labor and activity people used to do, they were burning off a lot of calories, so they didn't need to diet or go to the gym for exercise. Today, most of us engage in a fraction of the physical activity they did, yet we are probably eating about as many calories, if not more (and we're eating a lot of empty calories).

A report from the Center for Disease Control said that 80 percent of Americans don't get the recommended amount of exercise per week, which includes both aerobic strengthening and muscle strengthening. About 50 percent are meeting the aerobic criteria, but that still leaves half the population that is not getting the benefits of adequate aerobic exercise.[43] Too little exercise can have serious health consequences. For example, inactivity reportedly contributes to the same number of deaths as cigarette smoking.[44]

To provide more balance for your physical body, regularly engage in exercise you enjoy—walking, running, swimming, playing sports—making sure you get enough aerobic and muscle-strengthening exercise. Of course, consult your doctor before starting any exercise program. Here are the recommended guidelines for healthy physical activity for adults. (There are separate guidelines for children and older adults.)

+ For substantial health benefits, adults should do at least 150 minutes (2 hours and 30 minutes) a week of moderate-intensity, or 75 minutes (1 hour and 15 minutes) a week of vigorous-intensity aerobic physical activity, or an equivalent combination of moderate- and vigorous-intensity aerobic activity. Aerobic activity should be performed in episodes of at least 10 minutes, and preferably, it should be spread throughout the week.

+ Adults should also do muscle-strengthening activities that are moderate or high intensity and involve all major muscle

43. See https://www.cbsnews.com/news/cdc-80-percent-of-american-adults-dont-get-recommended-exercise/ and https://www.cdc.gov/mmwr/preview/mmwrhtml/mm6217a2.htm?s_cid=mm6217a2_w.
44. See https://www.cbsnews.com/news/inactivity-tied-to-53-million-deaths-worldwide-similar-to-smoking/.

groups on 2 or more days a week, as these activities provide additional health benefits.[45]

Besides the physical benefits, exercise releases positive endorphins in our body, generally causing us to feel better. Have you ever noticed that when people are depressed, they don't want to do anything or go anywhere? Refocusing our thoughts and getting busy doing something, like exercising, can lift our spirits.

Resting the Body

Additionally, we should work on getting enough sleep at night. General guidelines for adults aged eighteen through sixty recommend "at least 7 hours each night to promote optimal health and well-being."[46] This can be a challenge, but it will make a huge difference in our alertness and energy level. It will also protect our health: "Sleeping less than seven hours per day is associated with an increased risk of developing chronic conditions such as obesity, diabetes, high blood pressure, heart disease, stroke, and frequent mental distress.[47] Resting your body also includes incorporating the restoration principle we talked about earlier, giving our bodies, as well as our spirits and minds, regular "intermissions" for renewal.

CHALLENGE YOUR MIND

Mental Exercise and Entertainment

We not only need to exercise our body, but we also need to "exercise" our mind. If we don't challenge our mind regularly, our brain capacity can deteriorate, similar to muscles atrophying when they are not used. You gain and increase through use. You lose and decrease through disuse. And more and more research suggests that keeping our minds healthy is a lot like keeping our bodies in good shape.

---

45. "2008 Physical Activity Guidelines for Americans," US Department of Health and Human Services, vii, https://health.gov/paguidelines/pdf/paguide.pdf.
46. The American Academy of Sleep Medicine and the Sleep Research Society. See https://www.cdc.gov/media/releases/2016/p0215-enough-sleep.html.
47. See https://www.cdc.gov/media/releases/2016/p0215-enough-sleep.html.

All right, I know—thinking can be hard work! There are times when we just want to relax and not have to think about anything. I've been there. As we have seen, we all need times and days allotted to recreation and refreshment. And after a hard day at work, many people just want go home and watch television or browse the Internet.

That's okay—but don't stay there. Again, we need to keep things in balance. Hours in front of the television or computer screen each night will not be a benefit to us. We have to measure the importance of our activities, and we often put too high a priority on being entertained in ways that disengage our minds. There have been times when I have planned an entertaining activity, but then I was presented with another opportunity that was of greater benefit—something that would add real value and power to my life—so I set aside the entertainment in order to do the other activity because it had more worth and significance to me. We have to determine the proper investment of our time, energy, and efforts. That is what balance is all about.

Let's not allow our minds to languish by neglecting to engage them. People who are retired have to be especially careful about this. When you stop working full-time, or when you're not involved in daily activities that use thinking skills, you have to make a special point to use your mental faculties in order to keep your mind sharp now and into your latter years.

YOU GAIN AND INCREASE THROUGH USE. YOU LOSE AND DECREASE THROUGH DISUSE.

Stimulating Your Mind

The following are some practical things you can do to stimulate your mind:

Read. Back in the seventeenth century, English writer Joseph Addison said, "Reading is to the mind what exercise is to the body." He knew then what researchers are telling us today about the importance of keeping our mind in shape. I suggest setting a personal reading goal for each day, each week, each month, and each year. Apparently, if you read just fifteen minutes a day and then thirty minutes on the weekend, you can complete about twenty-three full-sized books over the course of a year. Some people enjoy joining a book club because it keeps them accountable to read and enables them to discuss what they have read with others. In addition, I recommend creating a short list of information-rich journals and magazines in your area of interest and setting a time to read them to broaden your knowledge.

Research. Research topics of interest to you in the areas of your expertise, ability, or particular concern. This will not only stimulate your mind but also enable you to stay sharp in your field. Don't allow yourself to slip into a rut, following the same procedures that you always have. Find out whether there is anything new and innovative being developed that relates to your calling and field.

Write. Keep a daily journal, writing down your thoughts and impressions. Journaling reportedly has the following benefits: it enables us to clarify our thoughts and feelings, know ourselves better, reduce stress, solve problems more effectively, and resolve disagreements with others.[48] Additionally, I suggest writing meaty, thoughtful letters to your most important contacts in life and vocation. You might write about what you have gotten out of your recent reading and research. Write about any helpful and interesting information you have gained that can benefit others as it has benefitted you. Another reason to do this is that when you discuss what you are learning, it will help clarify and reinforce the information to you. It will serve to strengthen your comprehension and absorption of the material, enabling you to better apply it to your life.

Learn a new skill. Take a course or a workshop in something that interests you intellectually or creatively. You might sign up for a community education course sponsored by a local college, or a class offered by your municipality or church; or you might create your own informal group of friends to learn something new together.

---

48. Maud Purcell, "The Health Benefits of Journaling," Psych Central, https://psychcentral. com/lib/the-health-benefits-of-journaling/.

Learn a new language. Language courses are often offered through community education programs, cultural or ethnic groups, or online. You can also learn languages through instructional books and audio recordings.

Memorize. You can stimulate your mind by memorizing passages of Scripture, literature and poetry, great speeches, quotes from well-known people, and even jokes. When we memorize and meditate on words, we engage our mind. And, while it starts with our mind, it will go down into our heart.

Listen. Build a collection of books, teachings, and study courses in audio format that are especially helpful to pursuing your purpose or stimulating your mind, and review them periodically.

Develop a hobby. Cultivate a hobby that engages your thinking skills, such as doing crossword puzzles or Sudoku, or playing chess or Scrabble. If you don't know anyone with whom to play chess or Scrabble, utilize electronic or online versions. Or connect with a relative or friend in another city by playing chess by e-mail or text.

THE BALANCE OF PROSPERITY

One of Jesus's closest disciples wrote in a New Testament letter, "I pray that you may prosper in all things and be in health, just as your soul prospers."[49] You will gain tremendous benefits when you grasp the importance of balance in your life and start putting these guidelines into practice. Becoming a person of balance will lead you to greater calmness, health, self-respect, and fulfillment in life. As I wrote previously, prosperity is not just about having all the bills paid, with money to spare in the bank. It is about having a peaceful spirit, a healthy body, a sound mind, and harmonious relationships with others.

BENEFITS OF A WISDOM-DRIVEN LIFE

+ Focusing on both personal renewal and personal growth will facilitate vital balance in our life.

+ The "slingshot principle" says that if we will pull back one day a week, the other six days will be more effective.

---

49. 3 John 2.

- The more we nurture our spirit, the better life we will have and the greater peace we will gain.

- Three major ways in which we can strengthen our body are by nourishing it, exercising it, and resting it.

- Becoming a person of balance leads to greater calmness, health, self-respect, and fulfillment in life.

APPLYING WISDOM

1. Which area or areas of your life could use more balance right now? Why?

2. Do you take time each week for personal renewal? How might you incorporate the "slingshot principle," or the principle of "intermission," into your life more fully?

3. List one idea for each area of personal growth—nurturing your spirit, strengthening your body, and challenging your mind—that most caught your attention in this chapter. Make a plan to take a small step toward integrating it into your weekly schedule.

13

WISDOM IS CONTENT

"Circumstances are the rulers of the weak;
they are but the instruments of the wise."
—Samuel Lover

In the next two chapters, I want to talk about additional ways we can advance true prosperity in our life. One way is by cultivating personal contentment, regardless of the circumstances we are facing or whether life is going the way we planned. The first step is to understand what true contentment is—and what it is not.

WHAT IS CONTENTMENT?

CONTENTMENT IS DIFFERENT FROM HAPPINESS

Many people equate contentment with happiness, but it is much deeper than that—it transcends happiness. When we confuse the two, we just set ourselves up for disappointment. Happiness is a state of *doing*, while contentment is a state of *being*. Happiness always depends on "what happens," so if people don't act the way we expect, or circumstances do not unfold the way we want them to, we're not happy. Contentment, on the other hand, is based on our "contents." We can look at it in this way: happiness is always based on what is going on *around* us, but contentment is always based on what is going on *within* us. There's a huge difference between the two.

Here are a few ways in which people miss out on contentment by becoming fixated with the idea of happiness.

HAPPINESS IS A STATE OF *DOING*, WHILE CONTENTMENT IS A STATE OF *BEING*.

Believing the "If Only" Myth

Some people live according to the "if only" myth:

"If only I *had* _____, I would be complete."

"If only I *was* _____, I would be happy."

"If only I *were given* _____, I would be satisfied."

"If only I had *a different* _____, I would be content."

Or they might get caught up in "destination disease":

"If only I were *promoted to* _____, I would be successful."

"If only I *lived in* _____, I would have a better life."

"If only I *could visit* _____, I would be fulfilled."

None of these scenarios, if fulfilled, would lead to real satisfaction because they are dependent upon external conditions or circumstances, which are changeable, or because they are based on qualities we might not be able to sustain. Until we make peace with who we are, and make peace with our past, we will never be content with what we have or what we may receive.

Having a "Good Times" Mind-Set

Other people miss out on contentment because they have a "Good Times" mind-set. If the good times are rolling, they are happy. If money is coming in, they are happy. If they have a significant other in their life, they are happy. If they are treated well, they are happy. If they are in a good mood, they are happy. If any of those conditions is missing, or flawed, they are unhappy—or even miserable—and they often let others know about it. Some people have the idea "I *deserve* to be happy," so when they don't get what they believe they ought to have, they are offended, and they think that someone else should provide it for them.

Thus, with the "Good Times" mind-set, people want ideal situations and circumstances, with everything working out in a kind of fairy-tale existence. For example, when they get married, they expect to live "happily ever after"—never having any conflicts with their spouse. Or when they plan a trip, they imagine everything will go smoothly—with no flat tires or missed flights.

We are setting ourselves up for failure big-time if we base our happiness on circumstances. What will we do if the job we love is eliminated, and our financial well dries up? We were on top of the world, living big, but now we have to downsize. Is material wealth really going to be the basis of our contentment in life? We have to realize we're going to deal with some up times and some down times. "Smooth seas never made a skillful sailor." We must have a strength inside us that will keep us from imploding when the world begins to put pressure on us on every side.

Putting the Power of Our Happiness in the Hands of Others

Some people place their happiness entirely on how other people respond to them, and they wear themselves out trying to make sure the people around them are always pleased with them. Or, they look to one person alone to make them happy in life. We can't rely on other people to make us feel good about ourselves. When we put our happiness in the hands of another human being, it is only a matter of time before they will disappoint us. They might not mean to do it, but they will let us down. It's just human nature. And even if certain people don't like us, it doesn't have to affect our peace, our self-worth, or how we pursue our purpose.

Therefore, *happiness* comes from other people treating us well, and from circumstances flowing in our favor. But *contentment* is about being satisfied with who we are. It comes from knowing that God is in control, regardless of our circumstances, and that we can have fulfillment in life even if we don't have everything we might desire or if we can't do everything we might want to do. Contentment is about adjusting our perspective and our attitude so that situations don't break our spirit before we are able to move beyond them.

We can't control what happens *around* us, but we can control what happens *in* us. Contentment is thus a state of mind, and it is a spiritual disposition rather than a state of achievement or of possession or of condition.

HAPPINESS IS ALWAYS BASED ON WHAT IS GOING ON AROUND YOU, BUT CONTENTMENT IS ALWAYS BASED ON WHAT IS GOING ON WITHIN YOU.

CONTENTMENT IS DIFFERENT FROM COMPLACENCY

It's important to recognize that living in a state of contentment doesn't mean that we are passive or indifferent toward life. It is not about accepting the status quo. It is not an endorsement for apathy where you don't ever try to do better, where you give up growing and improving. That is complacency, not contentment.

Complacency is defined as "self-satisfaction especially when accompanied by unawareness of actual dangers or deficiencies."[50] Complacent people are unaware that if you stay on the same level while the world continues to move, you will lose ground. For example, they may have a low-paying job, but they say, "I'm doing okay. I have a job, and I have insurance. Why

---

50. *Merriam-Webster's 11th Collegiate Dictionary*, electronic version, © 2003.

should I try for anything more?" In contrast, every truly contented person experiences what I call "inspirational dissatisfaction." The contented person is satisfied with what they have—but they are also looking forward expectantly to moving to the next level. The paradox is that we can be content and dissatisfied at the same time.

A complacent person and a contented person may work at the same company doing the same type of job. The complacent person accepts things as they currently are as a fact of life; they believe this is the way things are always going to be. Thus, they may tell the contented person, "Just accept the situation and give up, like everybody else. Accept that you are going to work like this for the rest of your life and that you are going to retire from this place." Many people remain in such situations because, as we have seen, we never change what we are willing to tolerate. However, the contented person believes the job is just temporary and that they will be moving on to greater things. That is why the contented person will become a supervisor while the complacent person will remain in the same position. In fact, the complacent person might even train his new supervisor.

Accordingly, even though we are content in our current situation, we ought to have our eyes on something greater. When times are difficult, what gives us contentment is knowing that we won't have to stay in that situation. We can say, "Even though things are not ideal right now, I am okay. I am working on something else, and I am doing what I have to do until I can do what I want to do." Contentment is based on perspective. Again, your outlook determines your outcome.

I believe that if we will learn how to be content where we are, faithfully doing what we have to do, while looking ahead to where we want to go, we will move forward. So do the best you can and be content on the level where you are. (If you are *not* doing the best you can on the level where you are, don't be content, because then you will not bring about the desired change!)

There may be times when things never seem to change. And whenever situations do not change, it is all the more necessary that *we* change—our attitudes and our perspectives—focusing on what is most important in life. We must learn to be content where we are, in the midst of our circumstances.

CONTENTMENT CAN BE LEARNED

Contentment is not a natural human endowment; it's not inherent in us. Neither is it a product of environment. There are many people who have lots of material possessions but are still not content. The reason some people try to surround themselves with all the external accoutrements of life is that they are using them as their security blanket. You can go to poverty-stricken countries in the world today where the average annual income is $250 a year and you will find some of the most contented people you have ever seen! I am an eyewitness to the fact that contentment is not based on material prosperity. Someone has said, "Happiness is not having what you want; happiness is wanting what you have."

Contentment is something we can learn. It is something we can grow and mature into. We have to learn how to be content when we have nothing *and* when we have everything. And although we might not like the idea, we often learn the lessons of contentment by experiencing its antithesis—discontentment, or even sorrow. Contentment is a choice that we make as we go through experiences that seem counter to the very lesson we are trying to learn.

New Testament writer Paul said, "I have *learned* to be content whatever the circumstances."[51] This comes from a man who suffered a great deal in his lifetime.[52] Despite everything that is going on in the world, and whatever surprises life brings us, we can live in contentment. A wise person learns how to use circumstances to help them grow. In fact, after we have gone through some difficult times, we may get to a point where things that used to bother us don't bother us as much. We can even transcend some of the things that used to really get under our skin. It's because we've been through these things before and found our way to the other side of them, and we know we can do it again.

Contentment will never be automatic for us because there will always be things that pop up in our life that cause us to begin worrying, that try to rob our joy and strip away our peace from us. They will try to distract us

---

51. Philippians 4:11 (NIV), emphasis added.
52. See 2 Corinthians 11:23–28.

from the purpose and provision of God and make us doubt our calling. But we can rise above all that worry and doubt.

If we can learn contentment, nothing will be able to keep us from living the life we were meant to live. Contentment is an attitude. It is a disposition of our spirit. It's not something contingent that says, "Well, it's raining today, so I am going to be sad." Contentment says, "Weeping may endure for a night, but joy comes in the morning."[53] Contentment says, "And let us not grow weary while doing good, for in due season we shall reap if we do not lose heart."[54]

Contentment always has something positive and hopeful to say. If we cultivate contentment, it will give us a positive message that will both encourage us and change our perspective. Contentment will not rise up from within us during difficult times if we have never made a point to learn it. But when we learn to be content no matter what situation we find ourselves in, something powerful will happen in our lives.

IF WE CAN LEARN CONTENTMENT, NOTHING WILL BE ABLE TO KEEP US FROM LIVING THE LIFE WE WERE MEANT TO LIVE.

CULTIVATING CONTENTMENT

To a certain extent, we each learn contentment in our own way, because the circumstances we face are unique to us. Yet there are some powerful keys that can help us to cultivate contentment in our life.

DEVELOP A POSITIVE PERSPECTIVE

To learn contentment, we have to develop a positive perspective toward life. We can't continue thinking life is against us or that things will always

---

53. Psalm 30:5.
54. Galatians 6:9.

remain the same for us. When circumstances get difficult, we need to give ourselves a mental thumbs-up. I have a great image in my mind of the way my father used to jog. He would always run with both thumbs up. It was as if the positive attitudes within him just had to express themselves physically. It's actually very difficult to think negatively when your thumbs are up. I can't explain it, but it just seems as though that thumbs-up gesture is connected to our thoughts. It triggers the idea, "Everything is all right. I'm going to be okay." We know that our thoughts have the ability to lift us up to another level. When we change our thinking, we give ourselves a mental thumbs-up, and it makes us rise up in our attitude, rise up in our determination, rise up in our willpower, and rise up in our commitment.

I have never allowed myself to become depressed over situations. Of course, I have had many great *opportunities* to become depressed. But each time, I have learned to turn that opportunity down. I am just not willing to give other people or circumstances that much control over my life. As someone has said, "I am convinced that we are as happy as we make up our minds to be."

To use a small example, sometimes when I am at a speaking engagement, something will go wrong, like a technical glitch, and the host becomes very concerned about how I am doing. They ask if I'm okay. Of course, I'm okay. I have learned to be content. If the microphone malfunctions, that's all right. I'm not going to complain about it or become offended. I know how to make myself content in whatever situation I find myself.

Paul, who had learned to be content in all circumstances and conditions, gave us a real key to contentment when he wrote,

Whatever things are true, whatever things are noble, whatever things are just, whatever things are pure, whatever things are lovely, whatever things are of good report, if there is any virtue and if there is anything praiseworthy—meditate on these things.[55]

This advice works in conjunction with the principle that whatever you give your attention to, you will create more of. Negative thinkers produce negative behavior, and positive thinkers produce positive behavior. Again,

55. Phillippians 4:8.

contentment is not inherent; we have to learn it. We can practice thinking about positive things, true things, good things, pleasant things, noble things. If we internalize such thoughts, we will produce them in our life.

PRACTICE THE ALPHA AND OMEGA PRINCIPLE

The Alpha and the Omega principle simply means to live every day as if it was your first day doing something new, or your last day completing something significant. We have an enthusiastic joy when we begin something we're excited about. And we have a satisfied joy when we finish certain phases and ventures in life. At those times, we seem to be completely in the present moment, and we have the sense that we are living life to the fullest. Each moment has value, and each moment is a celebration.

For example, think about how you felt when you first fell in love. You came alive, and you felt content inside—live just like that! Now remember how you felt on a significant occasion marking a "last" day. I can think of some school-related examples: the last day of school before summer vacation, the last day of exams before Christmas break, the day you graduated from high school or college. We often feel great satisfaction after having finished a substantial task or having completed a significant achievement. This may also be accompanied by the anticipation of starting a new phase in life.

Of course, your alpha and omega times might be different from these examples, but think about occasions that represent each one of them for you, and begin to live each day with the same kind of joy and satisfaction.

LOOK AT LIFE WITH GRATITUDE AND THANKFULNESS

Another great key to learning contentment is to live with gratitude and thankfulness. Gratitude is much more than an obligation of ritual politeness. Gratitude is a way of looking at the world that does not change the facts of our life but has the power to make our life more enjoyable. We can be thankful for what we already have, rather than dwelling on what we don't have. We can give thanks for the good things in our life. If we are able to make it through today, we can be thankful! We might be surprised at how contented we can be in situations where we don't have much. Contentment is a choice, not a circumstance. When we have the right attitude, we choose to celebrate life even in the midst of difficulties and uncertainties.

We have to prepare ourselves for the season that we are in. For example, we may go through phases and periods where money is tight. That's not the time for us to get bent out of shape. That's the time to say, "Lord, I thank You for my 'daily bread.'"[56] We have to learn to become thankful for our provision day by day until things turn around. I believe that if we are faithful and content with our daily provisions, we will come to a place of abundant blessings. We can say, "You know what? I may not have everything I want or need, but I am grateful for what I do have. My life may not be perfect, but I know there are others who are in a worse situation than what I'm dealing with." The real basis of contentment is having someone or something to love, something to hope for, something to be enthusiastic about, something to do.

THE REAL BASIS OF CONTENTMENT IS HAVING SOMEONE OR SOMETHING TO LOVE, SOMETHING TO HOPE FOR, SOMETHING TO BE ENTHUSIASTIC ABOUT, SOMETHING TO DO.

There is an Estonian proverb that says, "Who does not thank for little will not thank for much." You can tell the heart of a grateful person by how thankful they are over little things that are done for them. If someone doesn't thank you for the little things, they will probably get to a point where they won't thank you for the big ones, either.

I heard a story about the crash of a small plane at an airstrip in California in which the pilot was able to evacuate just before the plane burst into flames. A reporter asked him, "What in the world was going on

---

56. See, for example, Luke 11:3.

in your mind as the plane neared the ground?" He responded, "I realized that I had not thanked enough people in my life."

The things that ultimately make us content are the quality of our relationships—our internal integrity and peace, our relationship with God, and our relationships with our family and friends.

CELEBRATE LIVING SIMPLY

A surefire way to become content is to live simply and to appreciate the everyday joys. Simplicity is the essence of life. Learn to enjoy a sunny day or a quiet evening. I learned the principle of simplicity as I was growing up. My parents had six sons, and we had this saying on our wall: "My house is clean enough to be healthy and dirty enough to be happy." Our family didn't wait for special occasions to bring out the expensive china and eat in the dining room. Why have something that is valuable and then use it so little? Why turn a china cabinet into a shrine? We pulled the china out of the cabinet and used it to celebrate our life together. I can't tell you the peace, love, joy, and contentment that was within the walls of our house by the simplicity of our living.

We need to see that contentment is not about getting grand and sophisticated things and then saving them only for special occasions. Celebrate life daily with your family and friends. Celebrate your love for one another. You can't put a price tag on that.

GIVE OF YOURSELF TO OTHERS

As we have previously discussed, happiness in life does not come from what we receive; it comes from what we give. Here's a large reason why: When we receive something, all we have is what we have received—and the joy that comes with that lasts only for a short period of time. For example, if we buy a new car, we may be excited for the first couple weeks, but after a while, it becomes routine. The joy has no longevity. However, when we give to someone else and make their day, we receive the gift of joy that keeps returning to us every time we think about the individual and how they benefitted from what we did for them. Remember that even if we don't have a lot of money, we are rich in many other ways, and we can share with others our wisdom, knowledge, love, and support.

HAVE A GOOD LAUGH!

Last, but not least, we can cultivate contentment when we learn to just have a good laugh. Sometimes we take ourselves too seriously. We have to wear life like a loose garment and not allow ourselves to get so stressed out about things. When we have a healthy outlook, we know how to laugh at ourselves and how to laugh with others. For example, if you see bills piled up on your desk, and you don't yet have the money to pay them, you can quip, "You want what? By when? HA!" (To yourself, please, not to the payee!) It relieves the stress. You might make a point to regularly tell someone else a good joke, and enjoy laughing together. Additionally, it can be a good practice to read or watch something funny before going to bed, so you can relax enough to get a good rest. "A cheerful heart is good medicine."[57]

CONTENTMENT SEES THE BIG PICTURE

Please don't wait until you get a certain status in life before you are content. Please don't wait until you get a certain amount of money before you are content. Please don't wait until you get married before you are content. We are as content as we've made up our mind to be. Contentment has everything to do with perspective; it means having the right outlook because we can see the big picture—we are thankful for what we already have and what we are moving toward. When we really live in contentment at its highest and best, it doesn't mean we don't have problems or that we don't acknowledge them; it means that our problems don't have us.

BENEFITS OF A WISDOM-DRIVEN LIFE

+ We advance true prosperity in our life by cultivating personal contentment.

+ If we learn how to be content right where we are, faithfully doing what we have to do, while looking ahead to where we want to go, we will move forward.

---

57. Proverbs 17:22 (NIV).

- A wise person learns how to use circumstances to help them grow.

- Contentment gives us a positive message that will both encourage us and change our perspective.

- If we learn contentment, nothing will be able to keep us from living the life we were meant to live.

APPLYING WISDOM

1. In what ways might you have been depending on happiness rather than on contentment?

2. If you are in a difficult or undesirable situation, rather than resign yourself to the circumstances, how can you begin to look ahead and plan ahead for a better future?

3. Over the next six weeks, actively cultivate contentment by focusing on one key to contentment per week and applying it to your life: developing a positive perspective; practicing the Alpha and Omega principle; looking at life with gratitude and thankfulness; celebrating living simply; giving of yourself to others; having a good laugh!

14

WISDOM RELEASES THE NEGATIVE AND PROMOTES THE POSITIVE

"Reflective thinking enables you to distance yourself from the intense emotions of particularly good or bad experiences and see them with fresh eyes. You can see the thrills of the past in the light of emotional maturity and examine tragedies in the light of truth and logic. That process can help a person to stop carrying around a bunch of negative emotional baggage."[58]
—John C. Maxwell

We can advance true prosperity in our life not only by cultivating balance and contentment but also by addressing two common negative outlooks that can significantly hinder us. Many of the points in this chapter apply to other negative outlooks as well. When we address these issues, it will heighten our personal well-being as well as our professional pursuits and interactions with others. Releasing the negative and promoting the

58. John C. Maxwell, *How Successful People Think* (New York: Center Street [Hachette Book Group], 2009), 72–73.

positive is just as important to fulfilling our purpose as activities like plan-ning and goal-setting because it strengthens our ability to apply our plans steadily and consistently and for the greatest benefit to all.

It's not always easy for us to recognize (or acknowledge) when negative outlooks have crept into our lives. But as we talked about previously in rela-tion to habits, once we do identify something that needs to be changed, it's important to make a conscious decision to shed old ways that are impeding us and to take on new ways that will profit us.

THE NEGATIVE OF SELF-CENTEREDNESS

The first area I want to cover is the negative impact of self-centered-ness, something we all deal with in some form or another. For example, self-absorption can be a huge hindrance to us as we endeavor to use our dominant gift in pursuit of our purpose. I know gifted individuals who can't advance because they are focused chiefly on their own desires and on promoting their own contributions, and this turns people off. Such indi-viduals usually find few who are willing to help them further their goals. Thus, they find themselves trying to do on their own something they need others to help them accomplish, or to achieve in the fullest way.

A self-absorbed attitude isn't always so blatant; it can be quite sub-tle within us. In such cases, it may be *we* who reject the help of others who could further our goals. Sometimes, this happens because we sub-consciously want to receive sole credit for achieving something, especially when we've worked hard on it. Yet we cut ourselves off from the potential to accomplish something even greater and wide-reaching in cooperation with others.

RECOGNIZE THE WIDER HORIZON

As we have noted previously, there's a wider horizon than ourselves to consider, even as we pursue our unique purpose. Again, our God-given gift is not only for ourselves, but also for the benefit of others, or it's not a reflection of genuine purpose. Our gift is not primarily *for* us, although it is what gives meaning to our life, and we truly benefit from it. Rather, our gift comes *through* us to others. Our gift is the way we serve in this life, and its scope is larger than we are.

It can be hard to let go of the idea that our gift is not just about us. But John Donne was right when he said, "No man is an island entire of itself." We are not meant to be independent of others but interdependent. When we are successful at something, it adds value to us, but that alone does not bring *significance* to us. Our real significance comes when we add value to others—when we help to touch or transform other people, or lift them to a higher level in life.

LIVE ABOVE THE APPLAUSE

A symptom of self-absorption is to expect other people to constantly acknowledge our talents or contributions. If we wait for that to happen before continuing to pursue our goals, we may wait a long time. Let me just say that when your work speaks for you, don't interrupt it! We only waste energy when we focus on whether we've gotten enough credit or been recognized for our part—energy that could have gone into using our gift further or just enjoying the process.

We shouldn't become offended if others fail to appreciate us for who we are or what we have done. We must realize that many people around us will act selfishly and without appreciation, usually because of their own pain, their own frustrations, and their own unrealized dreams. At those times, we have to remember that it's not all about us but about our God-given calling.

In the Sermon on the Mount, in the context of charitable giving, Jesus said, "Do not let your left hand know what your right hand is doing…and your Father [God] who sees in secret will Himself reward you openly."[59] The same principle applies to the exercise of our dominant gift. While, as human beings, we all naturally need a certain amount of affirmation, we shouldn't dwell on that aspect of things because there will be an ultimate reward. My fulfillment is not based on somebody else appreciating what I do. My fulfillment comes in being able to say, "I did what I was meant to do." When God gives you the "well done," it's all worth it.[60] I'm grateful for those who can live above the applause, who don't need constant

59. Matthew 6:3–4.
60. See, for example, Matthew 25:21.

affirmation, who live for their purpose. There is liberty in just being who God called us to be.

> "IF I LIVE A FRUITLESS LIFE IT DOESN'T MATTER
> WHO PRAISES ME AND IF I LIVE A FRUITFUL LIFE
> IT DOESN'T MATTER WHO CRITICIZES ME."
> —JOHN BUNYAN

LET OTHERS TAKE THE LEAD AT TIMES

Sometimes, self-absorption manifests in disgruntlement if we think we should be in charge of something, rather than someone else. In these cases, we have to learn to yield to another person's leadership or authority. We should concentrate on who we are called to be, where and when we are called to be it. We don't always have to run things; we can allow other people to use their leadership gifts and to exercise their own callings. In fact, I feel wonderful when I am not in charge of something because then I don't have the responsibility for it! If I am called to take the lead in an endeavor or activity, I enjoy doing that, but if I am not called to be in charge, I just relax and am content to be a participant.

Be sure not to let a desire to be in charge keep you from participating in a project or venture with your best contribution. Additionally, don't allow it to prevent you from actively mentoring your children, your employees, your fellow members in an organization, or others in your sphere of influence so that they can learn, grow, and eventually be able to take the lead themselves according to their unique purpose.

When we understand all these things, we can release the negativity of self-centeredness and promote the positives of focusing on the wider horizon, living above the applause, and giving others an opportunity to exercise their own leadership gifts.

THE NEGATIVES OF ANGER, RESENTMENT, AND BITTERNESS

Anger, in itself, isn't necessarily negative; it's what we do with our anger that either hinders us or helps us. Anger is generally a response to an offense or a hurt. Unfortunately, many things happen in this world that wound or break people's hearts and cause them to become angry, such as being ignored, deceived, cheated—having their trust violated. When people express their pain, it comes out in angry words, but when they turn their pain inward, it can turn into depression. If we never resolve how we feel about those who have hurt or offended us, then our anger will degenerate into resentment. The resentment will fester into bitterness, and we will wind up with a bitter life. Bitterness destroys the human personality, making us cynical and egocentric human beings.

Some people become resentful because they feel that life in general has been unjust to them. Their dominant attitude is, "I can't ever get a break," and they are offended by other people whose situations in life seem to be better than theirs. They may resent another person for their success, thinking, *I don't know why they gave* him *that position. It should have been me!* As a result, they constantly react with anger toward other people or toward their circumstances instead of using their gifts to create something positive in their life. A resentful attitude will not win us many friends, and it will merely taint the exercise of our own gift.

WE HAVE TO ADDRESS OUR ISSUES AND
RELEASE THEM, CLEARING THEM OUT OF THE WAY
SO THAT OUR GIFT CAN FLOW FREELY
AND OUR PURPOSE BE REALIZED.

Let's not waste our time in resentment or bitterness. Doing so is like preparing a poison to use against someone else, but having it suddenly spill over onto us. It contaminates and burns a hole in the vessel that carries it rather than reaching the object for which it was intended. Instead, when we are caught in these negative mind-sets, we must learn to move past them, recognizing that we are only hurting ourselves. We have to address our issues and release them, clearing them out of the way so that our gift can flow freely and our purpose be realized.

EXPRESS YOUR FEELINGS

To address anger and resentment, we first need to express how we are feeling, but not necessarily to the person who hurt us or against whom we hold the resentment. Some people are hard to talk to face-to-face. They intimidate us out of saying what we really want and need to say. Sometimes it's not productive to confront someone. But we have to talk to somebody in order to get our feelings out. It is healthier to be outwardly angry in the right context than it is to internalize the pain, because again, that anger can eat us alive.

However, we should use wisdom in choosing the person with whom we talk. Many times, we feel most comfortable around people who share the same flaws we have. Why? It is because they seem to lend legitimacy to our feelings. There's no need for us to discuss the issue with them just so we can wallow together in anger or resentment. We should consult somebody who has been where we are and has successfully redirected their feelings into something constructive. As we have seen, if we spend time with individuals who value wholeness of body, mind, and spirit, and emotional health, it is likely that our body, mind, spirit, and emotional reservoirs will remain intact at the end of the day. When we cultivate relationships with balanced and positive people, we are almost sure to be more productive and enjoyable to be around than if we spend time with toxic people who reinforce negative outlooks that are contrary to our values and best interests.

Another way to express our feelings is to write them down on a sheet of paper, on a laptop or iPad, or in a journal. These methods are helpful because there are certain thoughts we might not want to express to another person, but we still need a way to let our feelings out. (Note that some of our thoughts might be so personal that after we write them out, we may choose to destroy what we have written, to protect ourselves or others.)

As I wrote in the chapter on balance, I think a journal is particularly useful because it is a private place for thinking through our personal issues, sorting through our feelings and experiences, or simply articulating our thoughts and dreams. The practice of journaling allows us to fully speak our mind; we can say whatever it is we want to express. You'd be surprised at how healing this practice can be. A study showed that after journaling about stressful life experiences, asthma patients on average improved lung function by about 12 percent. Additionally, arthritis patients on average found that their symptoms were 28 percent better.[61] Journaling is often a therapeutic process. We just can't permit our journaling to become so inward-focused so that we continue to harbor those negative feelings rather than releasing them.[62]

Another helpful method is to write a letter to somebody who has hurt you, even if you never actually intend to send it because, again, the intent is just to get it out of your system. The offender may no longer be alive, but you can still write that person a letter in order to express your thoughts, letting them know how you feel about what they did. The idea is that if it's written down, it's out of the mind. Many people have trouble sleeping because they are carrying anger or hurt in their minds and hearts. They're being tormented in the night by emotional baggage they might have released before they went to bed by writing about it. At such times, we can also express our feelings to God in prayer and ask Him to bring healing in the situation.

I recognize that there are certain hurts that run very deep, such as when people or their family members have been abused or molested, or when a relative has died or been killed. In these cases, professional counseling may need to be sought.

If we don't express our feelings in some way when we've been hurt, it can weaken us emotionally and even mentally, and it might even affect our health. Sometimes we walk around with the same wound, the same offense, or the same fear for years because we've put it in a room in our

---

61. See https://www.ncbi.nlm.nih.gov/pubmed/10208146.
62. See Steven Stosney, PhD, "The Good and Bad of Journaling," *Psychology Today*, September 6, 2013, https://www.psychologytoday.com/blog/anger-in-the-age-entitlement/201309/the-good-and-the-bad-journaling.

heart and kept it locked away, and it plagues our lives. We release it by confronting it, and we can begin to confront it by expressing it. Some people don't want to confront their feelings because they are afraid that they will react too emotionally, but it's all right to shed tears over our hurt or anger, because in doing so we can rid ourselves of toxic emotions.

FORGIVE OTHERS

After expressing how we feel, we need to extend forgiveness in order to experience full release. Remember this principle: the person we stay angry with controls us. They might not even realize they hurt us, and they are probably not even thinking about us. That person might not even be in our life anymore, but we're still bitter and allowing ourselves to be controlled by the individual or the situation.

Previously, we talked about how our programming creates our beliefs, our beliefs create our attitudes, our attitudes create our feelings, our feelings determine our actions, and our actions create results. When we forgive, we change our thinking about the situation, and this influences our attitudes, our feelings, and our actions, creating new, positive results in our life. Forgiveness leads to restored relationships. Thus, when a person loses the capacity or the willingness to forgive, they stifle their own relationships.

Jesus taught, "Do to others as you would have them do to you,"[63] and "Be merciful, just as your Father is merciful."[64] He was basically saying, "Treat other people the way you would want to be treated. Act toward other people with the same dignity and respect with which you would want them to act toward you." We show mercy to others just as God shows mercy to us because we know that everybody messes up sometimes. We're all going to make mistakes. We're not perfect people, so we all need mercy— from God and from other people.

Some people have been hurt so badly they don't think they will be able to forgive. There are times when we may ask ourselves, *Why in the world does God allow certain things to happen to us in the first place where we are put into a position to have to forgive?* God doesn't completely shield us from everything, but I believe He is *with* us in everything, providing comfort and

63. Luke 6:31.
64. Luke 6:36.

the ability to come through the experience stronger. And He can enable us to forgive.

Perhaps you have seen interviews with people on talk shows whose family member—mother, father, wife, husband, child—was killed by someone, and yet they express their forgiveness toward the killer. You may have wondered, *How on earth can you forgive a person like that? How are you able to do that?* If they didn't forgive them, they would forever remain a victim of the resentment or hatred within them, and their life would be full of bitterness. The killer would not only have robbed them of their family member, but essentially of their own life as well. They would be stunted in their growth as a person and in the fulfillment of their purpose. The same is true to some degree on any level of hurt we are dealing with. The only way to break that power is to release the offense from your life through forgiveness.

WHEN WE FORGIVE, WE CHANGE OUR THINKING, CREATING NEW, POSITIVE RESULTS IN OUR LIFE.

And forgiveness, like contentment, is something that can be learned. Like many things, forgiveness is a process and not an event. It doesn't usually happen overnight. You have to choose to forgive every time the memory of the offense comes back to your mind. You may say to someone, or about someone, who has offended you, "You hurt me, but I forgive you," and release the offense from your life. But hours later, or days later, or weeks later, the thought of what they did to you or a loved one may come back to your mind again, and you will have to remind yourself, "I have already forgiven them for this. I have already released it. I no longer hold it."

Thus, forgiveness is not usually a one-time act, especially with regard to deeper hurts. Every time the memory comes back, you have to release it again. But the more often you do that, the less frequent those instances will occur in your life.

When we choose to forgive, we are saying, "I am not responsible for what happened *to* me, but I am responsible for what happens *in* me. I am responsible for how I respond to it." If we make the right decisions about what happens in us, we won't become a resentful or vengeful person. We won't remain a victim. When we live with a victim mentality, we draw negatives into our life. But again, we break that power by saying, "I forgive."

Forgiving others includes learning to trust again. It's true that whenever you trust somebody, you make yourself vulnerable to being hurt, deceived, and taken advantage of; but it comes with the territory of trust. I would rather live with trust—knowing the risks—than to have no trust at all. I believe the person who trusts will make fewer mistakes than the one who does not trust, because trust is a sign of a healthy heart.[65]

When we forgive, we also need to be able to allow love back into our lives. Frankly, some people have been so wounded they don't know how to receive love again. I know a lot of people who have no problem giving out love, but they have a problem letting love in. Sometimes it takes greater humility to receive love than it does to give it. But we need a balance of both.

FORGIVE YOURSELF

There are times when we need to forgive ourselves as well as the person who angered us because of the negative way we have reacted to them. Moreover, it is not possible for any of us to be in a close relationship with someone and not have to forgive the other person and also be forgiven by them. We are inevitably going to offend somebody—sometimes knowingly, sometimes unknowingly. When we do, we need forgiveness ourselves.

Many people find it easy to accept God's forgiveness and other people's forgiveness, but they have the hardest time forgiving themselves. Yet we have no right to hold ourselves hostage to, and to continue to kick ourselves over, the mistakes and wrong things we have done. Guilt leads to feelings of inadequacy and unworthiness. For example, when people do something wrong, and then something negative happens to them, such as not getting

---

65. There will be exceptions to the amount of trust we should extend, such as in situations in which someone has abused us. In those cases, forgiveness is also needed, but we cannot trust in the same way. Depending on the situation, continued cautiousness or complete lack of contact may be necessary.

a job they wanted, they sometimes feel the result was justified because they are "paying" for what they did. Guilt can cause us to feel disqualified for our dreams and goals. The answer is to ask for forgiveness of others when we have wronged them, and to allow God to forgive and restore us. I regularly see God take the broken pieces of people's lives and put them back together again.

In his book *Choices That Change Lives*, best-selling author Hal Urban gives "A Top-Ten List of the Benefits of Forgiveness" that beautifully summarizes how forgiveness releases the negatives of anger, resentment, and bitterness in our lives:

1. Forgiveness brings an end to self-defeating behavior.
2. Forgiveness moves us out of the past.
3. Forgiveness sets us free and allows us to move on.
4. Forgiveness makes us better persons.
5. Forgiveness strengthens our character.
6. Forgiveness makes us more loving.
7. Forgiveness improves our mental and physical health.
8. Forgiveness gives us peace of mind.
9. Forgiveness increases our wisdom.
10. Forgiveness honors God [and releases forgiveness from Him to us].[66]

BENEFITS OF A WISDOM-DRIVEN LIFE

+ Releasing negatives that hinder us and promoting positives that upbuild us heightens not only our personal well-being but also our professional success and interactions with others.

+ Releasing the negative and promoting the positive in our lives strengthens our ability to apply our plans and goals steadily and consistently and for the greatest benefit to all.

---

66. Hal Urban, *Choices That Change Lives* (New York: Fireside Books [Simon & Schuster], 2006), 73–77. Bracketed portion added.

+ True significance comes when we add value to others—when we help to touch or transform other people, or lift them to a higher level in life.

+ When we forgive, we change our thinking, and this creates new, positive results in our life.

APPLYING WISDOM

1. What negatives can you identify as hindering your life? In what ways do you relate to the issues of self-absorption, anger, resentment, and bitterness?

2. How can you apply the guidelines in this chapter to release negatives that hinder you and promote positives that will up-build you?

3. Take a specific step toward releasing a negative and promoting a positive in your life this week.

PART 4
WISDOM FINISHES WELL

15

WISDOM TRANSFORMS DREAMS TO REALITY

"Now faith is the substance of things hoped for,
the evidence of things not seen."[67]

When we follow the wisdom journey, allowing it to guide us as we move from the conception of our dream to its reality, we progress through four main stages. Some of those stages are longer than others and involve repeated cycles, but each stage has a specific purpose.

FOUR STAGES OF DREAM TO REALITY

+ The first step is *declaration*. When we make a decision to do something and we declare it, affirming it to ourselves and others, we set our will in a particular direction. If we never decree anything, we will never get started. We are only committed to what we confess.

+ After we make such a declaration, we often immediately face opposition and other problems; this leads to the second step, which is *distress*. We wonder how we can possibly deal with all the obstacles

---

67. Hebrews 11:1.

and difficulties that seem to be working against the fulfillment of our dream.

+ If we are open to change and allow ourselves to be stretched, our distress will take us to the third step, *development*, which enables us to transition from one level to the next as we grow and mature. We may be a level-three person dealing with a level-five problem. Our problem is bigger than we are, so we find ourselves struggling. Yet here's the truth of the matter: while our problem is stationary, we are not. We learn to deal with the challenges of the level-five problem by developing spiritually, mentally, and emotionally. When we learn the necessary lessons, we eventually progress to a level four and subsequently to a level five, a level six, a level seven, and so on. If you're a level-seven person looking down on a level-five problem, you can now say, "That's not a problem," because you will have grown personally and professionally to the extent that you are greater than the problem and know how to address it, having outpaced it. Human beings have a marvelous ability to grow—we can grow personally, we can grow in our vision, and we can grow in the development of our gifts.

Remember that problems are normal to life and that every dream, every vision, will face challenges. I don't know anybody who has attempted to bring a dream into reality who didn't experience problems and need to discover how to deal with them. Given that obstacles and difficulties are to be expected, don't allow yourself to be pushed by your problems—instead, *be led by your dreams as you address those problems.*

Since we will continue to grow and develop throughout our lives, we will always find ourselves in this third stage in one form or another, but it will result in continual development, achievement, and success.

+ Our development ultimately leads to a *demonstration* showcasing our dominant gift. This is when the dream becomes reality—at least, the initial manifestation of it. We may have a number of manifestations of our dream as we go along. But our gift is not ready to be showcased until we have declared our dream, experienced the distress of difficulty and opposition, and submitted to the process of development. As we have previously discussed, our gift is inborn, but it doesn't function at its maximum capacity right away. We are to actively develop it, and we are to allow it to be challenged and tested before it comes to fruition.

OUR *DEVELOPMENT* ULTIMATELY LEADS TO A *DEMONSTRATION* SHOWCASING OUR DOMINANT GIFT.

To progress successfully through the above stages, we need to apply the principles of the wisdom journey we have explored thus far—discovering our purpose and dominant gift, making plans and goals, creating winning habits, cultivating key relationships, exercising sound financial strategies, overcoming procrastination, seeking balance and contentment in life, and releasing negative outlooks while promoting positive ones.

The following are some key points to assist you in putting these principles into practice as you progressively move toward your goal, carrying your dreams from original idea to fulfillment, even as you navigate the various mountains and valleys, the ups and downs, of this process.

1. KEEP THE DREAM ALIVE

The first point is to keep your purpose alive in your mind and heart by regularly envisioning your dream, by expecting the impossible, and by recognizing new opportunities.

REGULARLY ENVISION YOUR DREAM

Regularly envision what you want to accomplish and where you want to go, in order to keep your purpose clearly in mind and to allow that image to influence your actions. Doing so will continually reinforce what you have declared you will do. My father started carrying himself as if he was a millionaire before he ever became one. He had the mind-set of a millionaire, which influenced his thinking. Because he thought of himself as a millionaire, people treated him like one. After a while, the way he thought in his heart was manifested in reality in his life. Again, we always need to think toward the next level. Wherever you are in your mind is where you really are. Your actions will follow your thoughts.

EXPECT THE IMPOSSIBLE

Don't be afraid to expect the impossible. In fact, look for opportunities for the "impossible" to be realized! Take the story of Richard Montanez, a Mexican-American man who dropped out of high school due to language difficulties and took a job as a janitor at a Frito-Lay plant in California. The president of the company sent a message to all his employees encouraging them to "think like an owner." Richard was surprised that he seemed to be the only one in his department who began to take that encouragement seriously. After praying to God for an idea, he developed the concept for "Flamin' Hot Cheetos," which became the company's best-selling product.[68] Today he is an executive focusing on Multicultural Sales and Community Promotions for PepsiCo, the parent company of Frito-Lay. When you put a dream in motion, expect something beyond what you can see with your own eyes. Expect that doors will open for you. Expect that things will happen beyond your ability to calculate.

RECOGNIZE NEW OPPORTUNITIES

The ones who obtain the greatest benefit from a product or innovation are often those who spot its potential first or see its wider applications before others do. For example, when iPhones first came out, they were immediately popular and people were excited about using them. I thought they were wonderful, too, but I wasn't interested in having one because I already

---

68. See Nextshark, "A Humble Mexican Janitor Accidentally Invented Flamin' Hot Cheetos and This Is His Life," March 1, 2016, https://www.foodbeast.com/news/a-humble-mexican-janitor-accidentally-invented-flamin-hot-cheetos-and-this-is-his-life/, and Michael Ashcraft, "God Gave Hispanic Janitor at Frito-Lay Factory a Vision for Flamin' Hot Cheetos," April 11, 2017, http://blog.godreports.com/2017/04/god-gave-hispanic-janitor-at-frito-lay-factory-vision-for-flamin-hot-cheetos/.

had another type of phone that met my needs. However, I recognized their market value, so I purchased an iPhone—not so that I could use it, not because I was interested in its technology, but so I could open it up and identify its components and who manufactured them in order to know what companies to invest in.

If we don't recognize opportunities, we can't take hold of them. Accordingly, we should always look for opportunities to sharpen and hone our own gifts. Regularly review how you are exercising your dominant gift and look for ways to increase its effectiveness. What you were doing five years ago might be behind the times now. We have to constantly reinvent ourselves and stay aware of current developments so we don't become irrelevant in the society and time in which we live.

THE ONES WHO OBTAIN THE GREATEST BENEFIT
FROM A PRODUCT OR INNOVATION ARE OFTEN
THOSE WHO SPOT ITS POTENTIAL FIRST OR SEE ITS
WIDER APPLICATIONS BEFORE OTHERS DO.

2. FACILITATE THE DREAM

Next, we can facilitate the progress of our dream through pacing ourselves, acceleration, eliminating "dead weight," and moving past failure.

PACE YOURSELF

Life is not a sprint. It is more like a long-distance race where we have to pace ourselves. We must keep some energy in reserve and build up our endurance so that when we go through difficult challenges, we can still take strong and deliberate strides forward. Whenever we face a difficult experience, our tendency is to want to rush through it, to get it over with in a hurry. But we need to be more concerned with our development and endurance than with our comfort and convenience.

Pacing ourselves as we pursue our dream is necessary because we need time to prepare for its fulfillment. For example, suppose our character is not developed enough before our gift makes room for us in the world. Standing in the limelight often illuminates our flaws, and the imperfections of our character will be exposed. The question is, can we take the heat of exposure? We can if we will pace ourselves, allowing our character to be refined even as we continue to develop our gift.

Life is something that is lived forward; therefore, we can usually understand it only when we look back at what we have experienced and the outcomes of our actions. When we review the past, we can sometimes see why we needed to go through various difficulties to reach our goal. It may have seemed that we were moving toward our purpose in a roundabout way, but upon reflection, we see that our path allowed us to learn significant things about ourselves and our purpose as we walked the journey of life.

ACCELERATE THE PROCESS

There is a time for preparation and waiting, but there is also a time for acceleration. When it seems the right time to move forward, you may need to find a catalyst, a means of momentum, that will give you the ability to progress. How can you accelerate what you are doing and where you are going? It might require following through on or revisiting principles we discussed earlier: Spending time with individuals who are working in the same field, so that you can be inspired by them with fresh enthusiasm and insights. Or finding a mentor who has been where you are and can share their experiences and wisdom. Or clarifying your vision and making sure your goals are specific enough. Any of these things can serve to accelerate the manifestation of a dream. Review the wisdom principles to see where you might need to implement a step or revisit one.

REMOVE THE "DEAD WEIGHT"

Sometimes, circumstances or other people can hold us down like weights as we endeavor to develop our vision. These are weights that are wasting our time, draining our energy, or sapping our resources. Unless we remove those weights, we will be delayed in seeing our dream come to reality.

One of my favorite illustrations of the need to remove what is detrimental or no longer helpful in order to fulfill our destiny comes from a saying of the Dakota Indians, who have passed their tribal wisdom down through the generations: "When you discover you are riding a dead horse, the best strategy is to dismount." When we stay in a situation longer than we should because we are used to it, or when we keep trying to implement a plan that clearly isn't working, it is as if we are attempting to ride a dead horse. At such times, we can be slow to dismount, even when the finality of the situation becomes obvious.

When some people find themselves in this situation, they whip the horse, trying to get it to move. But the horse is still dead; it isn't going anywhere. Other people offer the horse sugar cubes, as if it just needs a little more energy to get it going. Still others try changing riders to see if that will help. Then there are those who form a committee to study the dead horse to determine what can be done.

I sometimes see people who are in a situation that is obviously not going anywhere. It might be a relationship they believed was going to be "the one," a business idea, or another dream or ideal. They believed in the horse, hoped for the horse, and loved the horse. Now the horse is dead, but they deny that fact; they think that dismounting is equivalent to giving up, and they fear there will never be another horse for them to ride. It is as if they are wearing blinders, unable to see any other ways or possibilities, maintaining tunnel vision, thinking that what they are currently doing is the way it's always been and the way it's always going to be. They end up putting their life on hold when they should be moving forward.

Dismounting from such a situation takes wisdom, and it rarely happens without our having an intentional process in place of what we want to do next. But it begins with acknowledging a lack of forward momentum in our lives, when we discover that despite our efforts to try harder and smarter, or to fix something, we're still in the same place. Some people need to crash, figuratively speaking, in order to hear that wake-up call. Ultimately, we have to acknowledge that remaining in that place is not our desired destination—which is when we finally get off the horse. We usually end up kicking ourselves that we didn't dismount sooner.

In such cases, moving forward might be the hardest thing we will ever do, but it is necessary. Sonya Ricotti, author of *Unsinkable: How to Bounce Back Quickly When Life Knocks You Down*, says we should "surrender to what is," "let go of what was," and "have faith in what will be."[69] It takes courage to do that; it takes trust to do that. Yet when we do, we will be able to launch out and do something different—or do the same thing but differently. We have to stay passionate about what we are called to do—what we have been put on this earth to accomplish.

Let me add this comment: If you have something you know works, but doesn't seem to be moving forward, don't change the formula (horse); instead, change the audience. You have to go where you are valued, because it will release your gift in a brand-new dimension. Find the people who love what you have to offer. They are going to be glad they met you.

"SURRENDER TO WHAT IS," "LET GO OF WHAT WAS," AND "HAVE FAITH IN WHAT WILL BE." — SONYA RICOTTI

CONSIDER FAILURE TO BE TEMPORARY

While progressing from dream to reality, we will inevitably deal with various setbacks, mistakes, and even failures. Some failures naturally occur when we go through the process of trial and error as we try something new or experiment with something. Often, failure is linked to inexperience. But failure is always written in pencil, not in ink. Being defeated is usually a temporary condition. Giving up is what makes it permanent.

---

69. Sonya Ricotti, *Unsinkable* (Pompton Plains, NJ: The Career Press, Inc., 2015), chapter 2.

We shouldn't throw in the towel just because we've been in a situation where we have failed at something we've attempted. In fact, people who avoid failure also avoid success. Failure inspires winners. When you are following your purpose and get knocked down and experience setbacks, you ought to become known as the "comeback kid." Confucius reportedly said, "Our greatest glory is not in never failing, but in rising up every time we fail."

Failure often reveals an area where we need to be taught something. With this in mind, we should become the richest students of life, particularly in the areas where we're being challenged. Often, the greatest lessons we can learn are those we discover through the troubles we go through. We learn more from our failures than we do from our successes. The lessons are in the struggles, not in the victories. Every defeat, every loss, contains its own lesson for how we can improve our performance the next time.

Since we inevitably pay a lot for our education in the School of Hard Knocks, once we pass the tests and get our degree, let's not forget what we've learned. Let's take the knowledge, the wisdom, and the principles of those lessons and allow them to empower us for our future. Frederick Douglass said, "If there is no struggle there is no progress."

While some failures are the natural result of experimentation and trying new things, other failures, as we have previously discussed, come from a lack of preparation. It costs us when we make poor decisions just because we didn't take the time to think things through. Thus, if we fail due to a lack preparation, we need to take the time now to assess the situation. We have all heard the saying, "If at first you don't succeed, try, try again." That's good, but it skips a few stages. If at first you don't succeed, then stop... think...and analyze why it didn't work that time. Make adjustments, and then try again more intelligently, incorporating the appropriate knowledge, wisdom, and planning.

Still another type of failure comes from a weakness of character. Those who have experienced such failure need to acknowledge it and address it with a plan for releasing the negative and promoting the positive in their life while developing positive habits.

Regardless of the cause of failure, nobody likes how failure feels when they experience it. The important thing is never to link our failures with our essential worth as human beings. Many people struggle with "hidden failure." These are individuals who look like they are doing well in life, but they are silently beating themselves up because they associate their failure with who they are, with their identity. It is totally in error for anybody to ever say the words, "I am a failure." *Failure is never a person; it is always an event.*

When someone experiences failure, they may go through various stages of reaction to that failure, depending on what form the failure has taken:

1. Surprise or shock ("This didn't really happen, did it?")

2. Fear ("What am I going to do? What's going to happen to me?")

3. Anger and blame ("It's not fair! It's so-and-so's fault!")

4. Guilt over what they did ("I messed up badly"), or shame over who they are ("What will people think of me now? I can't face them.")

5. Depression ("I'm a bad person") or despair ("I'll never get over this.")

With any type of failure, the solution is not to get stuck in any of these stages. We can work *through* the shock. We can work *through* the fear. We can work *through* the anger and blame. We can work *through* the guilt. If we do this, we will not end up in depression or despair but will ultimately look at the failure as a learning process.

"MOUNTAINTOPS INSPIRE LEADERS,
BUT VALLEYS MATURE THEM."
—WINSTON CHURCHILL

As someone has said, "Your condition is not your conclusion." Out of your greatest failure can be birthed your greatest wisdom. So determine not to dwell on the times when you have failed. It's a new day. Step out of your past and into your God-given purpose.

3. EMBRACE THE COSTS OF THE DREAM

The third point is to remember that we must embrace the inevitable costs of our dream, something many people are not willing to do. Included in the costs are the need for sacrifice and the need for perseverance.

EXPECT TO MAKE SACRIFICES

There is no question about it: if we are going to build something significant in our life, we are going to have to learn to sacrifice. We will need to work hard. Our gift will never come to greatness through mediocre, average effort. Victory is always on the other side of inconvenience. We will also have to make difficult choices about what is most important to us. Ask yourself, "What am I willing to give up in order to see my dream become a reality?" Anytime we increase our focus on something, we must decrease our focus on something else. We can't major in everything.

Additionally, we must be willing to be set apart from other people who don't share the same level of commitment. Don't be afraid when your dominant gift leads you into lonely places now and then, because focusing on your gift will require dedicated time from your life. Sometimes, we may need to sacrifice our sense of security. We have to change our perspective so that we become more in love with opportunity than we do with security; when we do, we will pursue our gift even in the midst of uncertainty because we know there is something better for ourselves or for others.

KEEP PERSEVERING

When it takes our dream a long time to come to pass, when we haven't seen much happen, we may become discouraged and begin to lose hope in the dream. We might even become irritated when people try to give us words of encouragement about it! At such times, we need to stick it out, work it out, and follow it through. We can't bring anything to perfection or excellence unless we learn to follow through. And we will never progress beyond our level of commitment. Whatever you need to do to pursue your purpose—even if you have to work on your dream in an office created in a corner of your basement or kitchen, even if you have to convert your night-stand into a desk—do it by the grace of God, and stir up your gift!

Have tenacity. Keep on pursuing. Never give up. Endure to the end. Remember, it doesn't matter how you start; it matters how you finish. You may not know how it will work out, and you may not know when your dream will finally manifest, but resolve in your heart, "I am not going to give up!" As long as you hold on to your dream and continue to develop your gift, your gift will make room for you, and your dream will become reality.

BENEFITS OF A WISDOM-DRIVEN LIFE

+ Our personal and professional development ultimately lead to a *demonstration* showcasing our dominant gift.

+ Regularly envisioning what you want to accomplish and where you want to go will keep your purpose clearly in mind and reinforce what you have declared you will do, influencing your actions.

+ The ones who obtain the greatest benefit from a product or inno-vation are often those who spot its potential first or see its wider applications before others do.

+ "Surrendering to what is, letting go of what was, and having faith in what will be" can help us to remove dead weights in our life that are preventing us from moving forward with our dream.

+ Every defeat, every loss, contains its own lesson for how we can improve our performance the next time. Out of our greatest failure can be birthed our greatest wisdom.

+ As long as you hold on to your dream and continue to develop your gift, your gift will make room for you, and your dream will become reality.

APPLYING WISDOM

1. Be creative in finding ways to keep your vision in the forefront of your mind, such as posting in your home or workplace a one-sen-tence summary of your vision, an inspiring quote, or a meaning-ful photo or picture.

2. What "weight" might be holding you back from progressing toward your dream? Make a decision to "dismount the dead horse," developing an intentional plan for how to move on from there.

3. How do you usually react to your failures, whether they are from experimentation, lack of experience, lack of preparation, or a character flaw? Consider the various stages of reaction to failure and which stage you might be in now regarding a particular experience. Assess what went wrong and think about what lessons you can learn from it that will empower you for your future. Always remember that *failure is never a person; it is always an event.*

16

WISDOM LEAVES A LEGACY

The life that you live is the legacy that you leave.

When purpose matures, it is called legacy. This is because once our dream becomes reality—and even while we are still progressing through the development stage and learning life lessons—the wisdom journey directs us to look for others along the path of life to whom we can pass along our knowledge and experience, smoothing the way for them and enabling them to better navigate it for themselves. As we have traversed that path, we have gathered a treasure trove of wisdom principles, and we have much that we can share for the benefit of others. Additionally, we have accrued other resources that we can give as an inheritance of prosperity and blessing.

INWARD, OUTWARD, UPWARD, AND ONWARD

Our dream or vision is meant to travel in four directions: *inward, outward, upward,* and *onward.* This is the process of legacy. God gives us dreams, visions, and ideas; we receive and internalize them, carrying them inwardly. Then, as we progress from dream to reality, those dreams, visions, and ideas manifest *outwardly* in the world. After they manifest, we are to hold them *upward*—to "give" back to the Creator what He has given to us so that it can experience even greater growth; again, God gave us our dream, and He can do more with it than we can imagine. Finally, our dream and the wisdom principles we have gathered along the way need to be passed *onward*, so that their influence transcends our own lifetime. We build for longevity.

I don't want what I have learned or gained to die with me, merely to enrich a graveyard. God gives us our life for a wider purpose than that, and I don't want to hoard mine. I want to be able to sow the seeds of wisdom I have gathered. I want to be able to plant them in people's lives, so that the wisdom will continue to be of benefit by enriching others. There will be people, some of them not yet born, who will need to know the wisdom principles that I have internalized and that are directing my life. And I want to make these principles available to them not only so they can use them for themselves, but also so they can pass them along to still others.

WHAT IS LEGACY?

Ultimately, the life we live is the legacy that we leave. That means our legacy has already begun. Whether we realize it or not, our life is presently making an impact on somebody else who is watching us or looking up to us. We build our legacy every day. Thus, legacy is not only about the future; it's about what we are doing right now. Therefore, here's my question to you: What are you doing to build an *intentional* legacy that will have a positive impact on the lives of others? As I wrote earlier, when we are successful at something, it adds value to us, but that alone does not bring significance to us. Our real significance comes when we add value to others—when we help to touch or transform other people, or lift them to a higher level in life.

Every great legacy begins with one person. You can be a significant blessing in this world. Whatever type of riches God brings into your life—mental, emotional, physical, or spiritual—He will give you the opportunity to use to enrich others. For example, He will make you rich with encouragement so that you can enrich others with encouragement. As a result, what you have received will be extended through you to others in an impactful way.

In this chapter, I want to focus on two major aspects of a wisdom legacy: (1) The inheritances we intentionally pass along to succeeding generations of our family—to our children, grandchildren, nieces and nephews, and others with whom we are close. (2) The mentorship relationships we purposely enter into, as well as the training we give to others.

LEGACY IS NOT ONLY ABOUT THE FUTURE; IT'S ABOUT WHAT WE ARE DOING RIGHT NOW.

AN INHERITANCE OF WISDOM FOR OUR CHILDREN

I believe the world would be a far better place if young people didn't leave home until they had received sufficient wisdom from their parents to be able to operate successfully in the affairs of life. Too many people go out into the world ill-prepared; consequently, they make silly, avoidable mistakes. If they never gain the wisdom to learn from their mistakes and amend their actions, they and their descendants will likely keep repeating the same mistakes.

To avoid this scenario, we can leave a wisdom legacy for our children and future generations in three main areas: *wisdom about life*, *wisdom about worth* (values), and *wisdom about wealth*.

WISDOM ABOUT LIFE

Wisdom Is a Guide, a Guard, and a Gauge

The role of wisdom can be summarized as being a guide, a guard, and a gauge for our lives. As a guide, it directs us on the journey of life, helping us to stay on the right path. As a guard, it protects and preserves us, mind, body, and spirit. And as a gauge, it enables us to evaluate where we are in life, to recognize where we may have wandered onto the wrong path, and to see areas in our lives that we need to improve or enhance.

That is why, when we pass along wisdom principles to subsequent generations, it can become an incredible blessing for perpetuity. Every person must internalize wisdom for themselves. But the value of having a head start—of receiving a legacy of wisdom from a parent, grandparent, uncle, aunt, or family friend—cannot be measured.

Many children don't realize what their parents have gone through in life and how they paid a dear price to gain the wisdom they possess. When we talk to our offspring—whether they are children, teenagers, or young adults—about the wisdom we've learned, we can help them to avoid the mistakes, missteps, and failures we have made, as well as the grief and pain we have experienced. We can save them headaches and heartaches by telling them, "I have already been there and done that, and I know where that road leads. Here is the better way I have discovered." We can teach them at an early age how to seek their life purpose and develop their dominant gift. We can help them through challenging times by letting them know how we made it all the way through a similar challenge.

If we do not give our children something to live up to, they may fall for anything. They need wisdom as a standard of measure for their lives to help them evaluate and govern themselves. They need our encouragement. They need us to build up their esteem. This will save them much lost potential in life.

The great lawgiver Moses instructed parents to pass along wisdom statutes to their children, saying, "You shall teach them diligently to your children, and shall talk of them *when you sit in your house, when you walk by the way, when you lie down,* and *when you rise up.*"[70] Teaching our children portions of wisdom throughout the day will nourish the next generation with the principles of wise living. We can also plant seeds of wisdom in our children's minds before they go to bed so that their minds can meditate on them at night. Sometimes we allow a vacuous television show to be the last thing our children take in before they go to bed. Instead, we can read to them or talk to them about something helpful and encouraging that will uplift their minds and spirits. These are ways in which we can bridge and bless the generations with a wisdom legacy.

Use Wisdom Like a Pocket Watch

Passing along wisdom to our children needs to be intentional, but it doesn't always have to be direct. They will pick up much wisdom just from the way we live our lives. Openly conducting ourselves according to wisdom

---

70. Deuteronomy 6:7, emphasis added.

in their presence provides a natural invitation for them to seek out our guidance when they have a specific problem or question. And when they themselves ask for advice, they may be even more receptive to receiving it.

Truly wise individuals don't push their wisdom on anyone. Instead, people usually need to seek them out. Have you ever noticed that wise sages are not gregarious, boisterous people? They are never out there trying to show off what they know, because real wisdom comes with great humility; it is peaceful, gentle, and humble.

Accordingly, there are times when we should carry our knowledge and wisdom like a pocket watch. Most people don't wear pocket watches anymore, but there was a time when a well-dressed man would wear a three-piece suit with a specially-made pocket on the vest designed to hold a round watch with a chain attached. When he wanted to know what time it was, he would pull the watch out of the pocket, glance at it, and replace it. He didn't show off the watch all the time; all you would usually be able to see of it was the chain attached to the watch, not the watch itself.

THE VALUE OF RECEIVING A LEGACY OF WISDOM FROM A PARENT, GRANDPARENT, UNCLE, AUNT, OR FAMILY FRIEND CANNOT BE MEASURED.

So use your wisdom like a pocket watch in the sense that you don't need to show it off all the time; pull it out to show your children, grandchildren, and other family members when they ask you the "time." Think about how tiresome it is to be around someone who acts like they know it all. For example, you may mention one fact, and they have to mention five or six other facts because they want to demonstrate how much more they know than everybody else at the table. Let's avoid that syndrome when it comes to dispensing wisdom. If you have the right time (if you have gained true wisdom), inevitably, somebody around you will ask you what time it is. When that opportunity presents itself, share what you have learned.

Of course, the pocket-watch approach doesn't replace regular, intentional teaching about wisdom to our children; but it does give us a helpful guideline for using discretion and timing, and for gaining receptivity.

WISDOM ABOUT WORTH

In addition to wisdom about life, we are to leave our children and grandchildren an inheritance of wisdom about worth. This means teaching them what is truly valuable in life. Most important, they need to understand their significance as human beings created in God's image who have been given an inherent purpose and dream; this is the foundation for a strong sense of self-esteem.

People who don't know their value may throw themselves away for practically nothing. Whenever we don't understand the worth of something we own, we will discount it, neglect it, or give it away. Yet when we know the value of what we possess, we will cherish it and take care of it. The sad thing is that many people don't recognize the worth of something until after they have lost it. But when we help our children to understand their intrinsic worth at an early age, they can learn to cherish it, thus gaining a solid footing for their life.

Teenagers especially need to have a sense of purpose for their lives. They are pressured by our culture to focus on superficiality and to constantly be occupied by forms of entertainment. Without a legacy of wisdom, it will be easy for them to fall into living irresponsibly, even dangerously. But if they have been taught their true value through wisdom principles, they can recognize that they have a unique calling and gifting by which they can contribute something great and positive to the world.

WISDOM ABOUT WEALTH

Third, we are to pass along an inheritance of wealth—and the wisdom to go along with it. Our material wealth is the sum of the money, property, investments, and other goods we have accrued, which blesses our life and the lives of our children and our fellow men. As we have discussed, we don't build wealth solely for the purpose of enjoying ourselves. Our real goal in life should be to *enrich*, not just to be rich. We ought to say, "God, help me to enrich others with what You have given me." Few people are going to get excited over the wealth you have amassed in this world. What will excite people is the good you have done with what you have amassed.

You never leave wealth to the next generation without also leaving the wisdom to understand it and handle it well, because, again, wealth always has a purpose beyond itself—the betterment of others. If those who inherit wealth don't have the wisdom to handle it, their use of it will be unproductive at best and wasteful or hazardous at worst. Too many people are interested only in inheriting money itself; thus, they pay no attention to wisdom that would enable them to manage their money in the best way. If someone doesn't understand the worth of their wealth, they will likely squander it very quickly, so that it never fulfills its purpose of blessing others. They will use it mainly to indulge their own desires, purchasing a lot of material goods for their own use, rather than channeling much of it into worthy endeavors. Moreover, they will squander the very means by which they could produce additional wealth.

Most parents do not take the time to share financial principles with their children that would help them learn to become effective stewards over their own resources and the resources they will inherit. We have a responsibility to provide this information so that, in the future, our children can make wise decisions for themselves and their families. Don't assume your children will automatically figure out how you manage your finances. They need to know how you handle yourself behind the scenes. You have to purposely and patiently teach them financial principles.

KNOW THE WAY, GO THE WAY, AND SHOW THE WAY

To create a legacy in each of these areas—wisdom about life, wisdom about worth, and wisdom about wealth—it is necessary to follow through on all three stages of following wisdom: the person who is wise *knows the way, goes the way*, and then *shows the way* to others. Some people know the way but never go the way. Others know the way and go the way, but they never show the way to anybody else. Truly wise men and women don't allow the way they have found to end with them; after they find their way through a door, they teach others how to come in, also, and do what they are doing.

In many different areas, my mother and father followed through on all three stages of wisdom—knowing the way, going the way, and then showing the way to their children. Today, I stand in the strength of the standards and principles that upheld them in their own lives, showing them how to live well and to remain resilient under all conditions. For example, they demonstrated how to survive the storms of life, so that, as I was growing up, I was being fortified to endure the storms I would face one day. That is why, today, I do not duck out or give up when times get hard; I have been prepared to handle turbulence. I appreciate people who go through storms like financial shortfalls, sicknesses, or business challenges and are able to say, "I can handle this. I am built for the storm."

We need more people who are committed to know the way, go the way, and show the way of wisdom—learning, applying, and sharing wisdom with others. Just remember: You can't lead where you don't go, and you can't teach what you don't know. We begin our wisdom legacy by practicing wisdom ourselves.

MENTORSHIP AND TRAINING

We can offer wisdom principles and wise perspectives in many different contexts, from casual conversations to workplace conferences to town council meetings. But another major way we can leave a strong legacy is by purposely entering into a mentor relationship with a specific individual or individuals—whether in the realm of work, church, volunteerism, or another area—to pass along what we have learned and gained. Many of us are able to stand strong today because of the support of those who have mentored us, whether in a formal or informal way. We can do the same for others.

REACH OUT TO SOMEONE

If it has been only five, ten, or fifteen years since you graduated from high school or college, you probably clearly remember how it feels to first get started in life and to have to learn those early lessons about work, responsibility, and relationships. Or if you have followed a vocation over the span of thirty or forty years, you know well what it's like to have to persevere and adjust to changing times. In whatever stage of life you are in, I encourage you to reach out as a mentor or a friend and provide wisdom principles to help somebody else who is just starting out or who is in the thick of life's challenges.

Remember, you might be able to impress people from a distance, but you can only ignite and impact them up close. You are not called to help everybody, but there will be specific people along your wisdom journey who will particularly benefit from your mentorship. Choose them intentionally and carefully, because mentoring is a special investment of your time and energy. However, the results will be significant and well worth the investment.

You might choose to mentor someone based on your empathy for them, because they are going through difficult times that are similar to what you yourself have experienced in the past; your heart goes out to them, and you want to help them to move forward in life. Or you might choose to mentor a younger colleague in your field or workplace. Or someone may come to you to ask for your regular guidance and instruction. When you mentor someone—whether in a formal or informal, general or specialized, way— there must be mutual agreement to the arrangement, so that it can be an approved, growing relationship. Sometimes, mentorship relationships can deepen to the point that the participants come to feel like they are family, as if they are connected through a similar DNA.

YOU MIGHT BE ABLE TO IMPRESS PEOPLE
FROM A DISTANCE, BUT YOU CAN ONLY IGNITE
AND IMPACT THEM UP CLOSE.

A PATTERN FOR MENTORING

Jesus modeled four main elements of mentoring when He trained His twelve closest disciples, giving us a clear pattern for developing our own mentoring relationships (this pattern also applies to passing along a legacy of wisdom to your children and grandchildren):

1. *Instruction.* Jesus taught His disciples foundational wisdom upon which to build a strong and wise life.

2. *Illustration.* We might also call this element *demonstration.* Jesus didn't just instruct His disciples, but He personally demonstrated what He taught. Remember, who we are often speaks louder than what we say. Usually, it is what we demonstrate and model for people that will be most clearly "heard" by them. The wise person does not merely say to the person experiencing a challenge, "Go on, you can do it." The wise person says, "*Come along* with me. I've been there, and I know what to do. Just walk in my steps."

(3) *Involvement.* Jesus gave the disciples the opportunity to put into practice for themselves what they were learning so they could gain experience. This is mentorship through hands-on opportunities.

(4) *Internalization.* Jesus encouraged the disciples to come to a higher level of understanding and maturation by allowing the teaching to become part of who they were. As we have seen, we must internalize something before we can manifest it. And we develop into who we are by a process.

When you mentor and train others with wisdom principles, it can yield many positive results in their life and in the lives of others in their sphere of influence. For example, I taught a thousand leaders in Africa through six sessions entitled "Training the Trainer." Each participant had to agree to teach twenty-five other leaders as a requirement for attending the sessions, which were held over a period of time. Thus, from those one thousand leaders, twenty-five thousand other individuals were trained, and they received booklets to be able to train still others.

This training was not something I was paid to do; I did it as an investment in others' lives, and my heart was touched to see how various individuals were impacted by it. A gentleman in his sixties told me, "I have a sixth-grade education. The training that you have given me here as a leader is the only formal training that I've had." Then he added, "I'm taking it and teaching it to two hundred and fifty other men." This man understood that he was being taught not only so that he himself could learn, but also so that he could teach others what he had learned. And that is how mentorship works. Those whom we instruct can impact many more lives as they become mentors and teachers themselves.

Never allow the wisdom you have gained through this book or any other source to stop with you. Share it with others. Then tell them, in effect, "What I have done for you, do for somebody else. I'm feeding you wisdom principles so you can plant wisdom seeds in another person's life."

Again, every great legacy begins with one person. What will your wisdom legacy be?

BENEFITS OF A WISDOM-DRIVEN LIFE

+ When we pass along our wisdom to subsequent generations, it can become an incredible blessing for perpetuity as a guide, a guard, and a gauge.

+ Teaching our children portions of wisdom throughout the day and before they go to sleep at night will nourish the next generation with the principles of wise living.

+ Openly conducting our lives according to wisdom in the presence of our children provides a natural invitation for them to seek out our guidance and advice.

+ When we teach wisdom principles and mentor others, it can yield many positive results in their life and in the lives of others in their sphere of influence as they become mentors and teachers themselves.

APPLYING WISDOM

1. Think about the implications of the statement "The life that we live is the legacy that we leave." Write down what you think your legacy is at this point in your life. Then make a specific plan to build a strong wisdom legacy as you advance your life purpose and goals.

2. In what ways might you more effectively teach your children or grandchildren wisdom about life, wisdom about worth (values), and wisdom about wealth?

3. Are you currently mentoring someone? If so, review and include in your mentoring the pattern for mentorship outlined in this chapter.

4. If you are not currently in a mentoring relationship, consider carefully and intentionally whom you might reach out to in such a relationship, and develop a clear plan for how you will go about it.

CONTINUING THE WISDOM-DRIVEN LIFE

KEEP PURSUING WISDOM

"Wisdom is more precious than rubies,
and nothing you desire can compare with her."[71]

The wisdom-driven life is an ongoing pursuit. Again, wisdom is a journey, not a destination. We should never stop learning wisdom but continue to gather it so that it can heighten our success in life and be used for the benefit of others.

Here are some guidelines and reminders for continuing to pursue wisdom principles. They are based on instructions Solomon recorded from his father about obtaining wisdom and keeping it the principal thing in life.[72]

1. *Seek out wisdom.* When we seek out wisdom, it is not a casual looking, like window shopping or idly surfing the Internet. It is a dedicated search. Think of wisdom as gold or diamonds, as something of great value that is worth making a dedicated effort to retrieve. You don't find gold or diamonds just lying around waiting for you. You have to dig for them,

---

71. Proverbs 8:11 (NIV).
72. See Proverbs 2:1–11.

explore for them. If I were to guarantee you that there was treasure hidden in your backyard, you would probably dig up every inch of earth, if necessary, to find it—even if you had just landscaped your lawn with Bermuda sod. And wisdom is much more important to us than any material treasure. Many people are surrounded by resources that can provide them with the wisdom they need in life, but they never see them because they aren't actively looking for them. We always have to be alert to learn wisdom that can improve our lives.

2. *Tune in to wisdom.* We can to train ourselves to tune in to the abundant sources of wisdom that are available to us in life. (See the section that immediately follows this one, entitled, "Use All the Sources of Wisdom.") Tuning our ear to wisdom will also enable us to focus on what is positive and will build us up rather than on what is negative and will tear us down. For example, it's hard to receive wisdom and live according to it if we are attuned to people who are always complaining about circumstances or criticizing other people. Misery loves company, and many people are looking for companions to join them in their negativity. Instead, tune in to the positive and constructive sounds of wisdom.

3. *Receive wisdom.* Don't allow the wisdom you hear to go in one ear and out the other, or overlook the wisdom that you see being demonstrated by others, or forget the wisdom you have learned through personal experience. Receive it into your life. You can't do anything with something you have not first accepted for yourself.

4. *Keep treasuring wisdom.* If we don't keep treasuring the wisdom we receive, we won't be inclined to consider its implications for our life, and we won't retain it for long. We will be like the person who holds a yard sale and puts a two-dollar price tag on a valuable antique or a painting by a famous artist that they found in their attic because they didn't recognize its worth. A discerning buyer or an expert who combs yard sales would spot such a treasure right away, purchase it, and immediately own a valuable asset. Let us treat wisdom like the priceless asset it is, even if others around us don't recognize its worth.

5. *Apply wisdom.* Application is the evidence of learning. We have to put into practice the wisdom we find, receive, and treasure. Some people

can encounter wisdom and never be changed by it. They might hear the very thing they need in order to address an issue or problem in their life, but they don't listen to it—or, if they do listen, they never implement it. As I wrote at the beginning of this book, if you don't take the time to apply wisdom to your life, then wisdom is really no good to you at all; you will gain none of its benefits.

6. *Ask questions to gain discernment and understanding.* You don't have to wait until after you are deep into a project, a pursuit, or a relationship to seek wisdom principles that can guide you in relation to it. Avoid jumping into anything without first thinking it through and seeking sound advice. When you apply good judgment from the beginning, you will save yourself much heartache, trouble, and failure. If you are facing an issue or problem, talk to those who can help you address it. Additionally, if you are having difficulty understanding or applying a particular wisdom principle, don't just continue to wonder about it but seek further clarification and assistance so you can put it into practice. Talk with a mentor, colleague, or friend. You won't know if you don't ask; and you won't move forward if you don't inquire of those who have more wisdom and experience than you do.

7. *Pass wisdom along.* Share the wisdom principles that you have found, tuned your ear to, received, treasured, applied, and gained a deeper understanding about. As we discussed in chapter 16, "Wisdom Leaves a Legacy," build an inheritance of wisdom assets that you can pass along to others, now and for posterity.

USE ALL THE SOURCES OF WISDOM

"Where there is no counsel, the people fall;
but in the multitude of counselors there is safety."[73]

The following are a review of some of the most significant sources of wisdom we can draw from as we continue to pursue a wisdom-driven life; together, they become our "multitude of counselors" for wise living.

OUR PERSONAL EXPERIENCES

One way we learn wisdom is through our personal experiences—with other people, and with life events. This might take the form of a pleasant or rewarding experience in which we learn that adopting a certain attitude or engaging in a particular practice brings a positive result, or it might take the form of an unsatisfying or uncomfortable experience in which we discover that adopting a certain attitude or engaging in a particular practice yields a negative result. Many times, we learn the right way to do something by doing it the wrong way the first time.

---

73. Proverbs 11:14.

Remember, as long as we learn something from a negative experience, it was not in vain. Experience, by itself, does not yield wisdom. Some people make the same mistakes over and over again and never benefit from them by understanding what went wrong and making a correction. But if we can learn something from a negative experience (as uncomfortable as it might be), it can be a very useful source for gaining wisdom.

THE WAYS AND EXPERIENCES OF OTHERS

We gain wisdom by observing or studying the ways of other people—those who lived in the past as well as those who live in the present, but especially those whom we encounter and interact with on a regular basis. We can learn from both their successes and their failures. One approach is to examine the ways of those who have already achieved what we are working toward, asking ourselves questions like, "What attitudes does this person exhibit while pursuing their vocation?" or "What are this individual's work habits?" If the attitudes and habits reflect wise living and achieve good results, then they should be learned and followed.

OUR PERSONAL CONVICTIONS AND STANDARDS

In the book *The Power of Character in Leadership*, Myles Munroe wrote, "*Values*, *ethics*, and *principles*…are the standards that a leader establishes for himself—and lives according to—in the process of exercising his potential and ability for the accomplishment of his vision."[74] As we discover and internalize wisdom principles, we develop standards and convictions for our life that we should continually review as a source of guidance and assessment.

CORRECTION, INSTRUCTION, AND CONSTRUCTIVE CRITICISM FROM OTHERS

Correction may not always be the most welcome avenue for receiving wisdom, but it is an essential one. In fact, receiving loving discipline from parents or other adults is often the first way people encounter wisdom in their lives as children.

---

74. Myles Munroe, *The Power of Character in Leadership* (New Kensington, PA: Whitaker House, 2014), 37. Emphasis is in the original.

By accepting helpful instruction, guidance, and constructive criticism from other people (including mentors, employers, teachers, and friends), we learn to understand and absorb wisdom. If we want to make use of this particular resource for wisdom, we will need to develop the quality of teachability and be willing to listen to correction where it is warranted. Many people lose out on wisdom benefits because they never want to hear they've done anything wrong or acknowledge that someone else may have something to teach them.

OUR CONSCIENCE

We may feel convicted in our conscience that something is right or wrong, wise or unwise; that we should do or say something, or not do or say something. This form of internal guidance and direction can reinforce the way of wisdom for us and encourage us to follow it.

We should recognize, however, that the conscience is not always foolproof. We might feel perfectly justified in following a path that is not right for us if, for example, we become overconfident or feel offended by someone who has wronged us. That's why it's so important to develop personal convictions and standards that can guide us in the best way to respond to a situation, regardless of our fluctuating emotions or motivations.

THE COUNSEL OF OTHERS

Another valuable source of wisdom, and often a safeguard for our life, is the counsel of people we trust and respect. As the quote at the beginning of this section says, "Where there is no counsel, the people fall; but in the multitude of counselors there is safety."

We should seek out good advice from others, hear what they have to say, and consider it carefully. Beneficial counsel can come from family members, friends, or coworkers; from professionals in various fields; from the teachings of authors and experts in books or on electronic media; and from other sources.

It's important that we not take advice from just anyone but instead evaluate the people whom we are considering looking to for wisdom. We can review what they have previously said and done to help determine whether they are trustworthy and reliable. Then, after we listen to them, we should weigh their advice. Moreover, no one person has the answers to all our wisdom requirements. We should consult various sources, especially on serious matters.

MENTORSHIPS, APPRENTICESHIPS, AND OTHER ASSOCIATIONS

Additional sources for gaining wisdom are mentorships, apprenticeships, and other associations; they may be in the professional, volunteer, religious, or community realm, or in another area. Perhaps there is someone in your line of business who has acquired wisdom you would like to tap into. You might invite them out to lunch one day and pay for their meal, asking them to give you advice and guidance to help you grow in your field.

In a mentorship or apprenticeship, you purposely align yourself with someone who has experience, wisdom, skill, or knowledge in an area you want to learn more about or develop in your own life. Perhaps there is someone in an occupation you are interested in pursuing with whom you could arrange an apprenticeship, whether formal or informal, in order to have regular access to their knowledge, methods, and advice. When we work alongside another person over a period of time, it enables us to absorb knowledge and wisdom from them.

THE NATURAL WORLD

Another source of wisdom, which many people overlook, is the natural world around us, above us, and below us. Solomon famously discoursed about the wisdom that could be gained by studying the ways of ants, who exhibit characteristics such as industry and planning for the future.[75] There are many things we can learn from observing the patterns of nature. The yearly cycle of natural seasons teaches us to expect periods of birth, growth, dormancy, and reactivation in the advancement of our dreams and in the cycles of our lives. Even the simple act of caring for a house plant can give us an object lesson in the need for ongoing nourishment and patience during the various stages of growth as we're working to develop mind, body, and spirit.

---

75. See Proverbs 6:6–8; 30:25.

INSPIRATION

I have known people—including myself—to receive wisdom they wouldn't have obtained any other way except by connecting with God's wisdom through inspiration. The wisdom sometimes comes as a sudden insight or understanding in which they know what to do in a situation.

We all have times when we are stumped about something for which we need wisdom. At such times, I especially rely on prayer and say, "God, I need Your help with this." New Testament writer James counseled, "If any of you lacks wisdom, let him ask of God, who gives to all liberally and without reproach, and it will be given to him."[76] I have received many answers to my prayers. Additionally, one of the primary sources of wisdom in my life has been the Bible. Paul wrote that "all the treasures of wisdom and knowledge" are hidden in God.[77]

Ultimately, I believe all wisdom comes from the Creator, even though it often comes through human "messengers" rather than directly. I think God frequently uses people as answers to our prayers. He gives us wisdom through a variety of sources, but He is the Giver.

---

76. James 1:5.
77. Colossians 2:3.

ABOUT THE AUTHOR

Dr. Dale C. Bronner is a wisdom authority, life-maximizer, legacy-builder, and inspirational speaker, equipping leaders from all walks of life with time-tested, relatable principles for personal and professional development.

Dr. Bronner is a member of the board of directors of John Maxwell's organization EQUIP Leadership, Inc. He also serves on the board of directors and is part owner of Bronner Brothers Manufacturing Company, Inc., a multimillion-dollar, family-owned corporation that has been in the hair care business for over sixty years.

For four decades, Dr. Bronner has studied, tested, and applied the principles of wisdom. With the insights he has gleaned in addressing the demands and opportunities of leadership, professional growth, and personal fulfillment, he has helped thousands learn how to realize their maximum potential. A leader's leader, he is author of a number of books, including *Change Your Trajectory*, *Planning Your Succession*, *Pass the Baton*, *Home Remedies*, *Treasure Your Silent Years*, *A Check Up from the Neck Up*, *Guard Your Gates*, and *Get A Grip*.

Dr. Bronner resides in Atlanta, where he leads Word of Faith Family Worship Cathedral, a thriving interdenominational ministry with more than twenty thousand members. He is also a bishop in a network of more than sixteen thousand churches. His daily international multimedia broadcast has a reach of millions.

He and his wife, Nina, are the parents of four daughters and one son, and the grandparents of two granddaughters and two grandsons.

www.DaleBronner.com/
Facebook.com/Bishop-Dale-C-Bronner/
Twitter @BishopBronner